Marcy,
I hope that y
a few pearls of va-
information in the pages
follow. God Bless.

ND[signature]

PRESS THE "FIX ME" BUTTON

IMPROVE YOUR LIFE THROUGH PERCEPTION MODIFICATION

DR. RICHARD A.M. POWELL

BALBOA.
PRESS
A DIVISION OF HAY HOUSE

Balboa Press books may be ordered through booksellers or by contacting:

Balboa Press
A Division of Hay House
1663 Liberty Drive
Bloomington, IN 47403
www.balboapress.com
1-(877) 407-4847

ISBN: 978-1-4525-3251-6 (sc)
ISBN: 978-1-4525-3255-4 (hc)
ISBN: 978-1-4525-3253-0 (e)

Library of Congress Control Number: 2011902470

Printed in the United States of America

Balboa Press rev. date: 2/18/2011

Gratefulness - Webster defines it as: Thankful.

I want to thank my wonderful wife Jennifer, our four boys as well as everyone that has been a part of the journey that has formed the experiences that brought this book to life. If it hadn't been for the experiences in my life there wouldn't have be a word written. Thank you.

TABLE OF CONTENTS

INTRODUCTION

It's amazing how life can transform you in a matter of seconds.

I never understood what people really meant when they told me that I'd better turn my life around – until I did. Looking back today, I wouldn't change a thing. Where I've been has brought me to where I am, making me *who* I am.

So, here you are.

Maybe you picked up this book because you liked the cover art or the title, or because a friend recommended it. No matter. You have the book in your hands, and you want answers. I don't know if you'll find what you're seeking here, but I'm certain that you'll walk away with a new outlook on life.

You may have carefully crafted your journey through life, but no matter what experiences you enjoy or endure, your *perception* of each and every event is what ultimately matters. Everyone tries to make sense of his experiences – just as a novelist tries to find the moral in every book he writes. Unfortunately, many people get trapped in the "who done it" part of their story, and lose sight of the moral.

That's where this book will help you.

Let's face it: We all live life, and sometimes life lives us. It's easy to get mired in the muck and drama. We try to get unstuck, but it often seems that something or someone holds us back. I understand that. I've been there. On some days, I'm *still* there. Like you, I struggle from day to day, trying to make the best of things, and on some days, life just sucks.

So why am I writing this book – someone who admits that his life is not an earthly paradise? And why should you bother to read it?

Since I was 12 years old, I've been told that my actions and behaviors were unacceptable to my family and society – that I needed to change my life's direction. There was just one problem: Nobody could divulge the secret to changing my life. I asked my parents, the neighbor, judges, corrections officers – everyone. They all offered the same stale reply, "I can't tell you how to change. You just need to do it."

That advice is like telling a baseball player that he *just* needs to hit a home run every time he comes to bat – vague and useless. I would have given 10 years of my life if someone offered me the answers I needed. I wasn't a bad kid. I just needed direction. What I didn't realize back then was that I *was* receiving direction – not from any one person, but from *life* itself. I was once told that events and experiences don't make us who we are. *It is the lessons hidden in our experiences that carve our future.*

What does that mean? It means that we have our own storylines. We have experiences that have been written into chapters and compiled into the book that is our life. Some of us have chosen to write a horror novel; others a self-help book. I don't have all the answers, but I *do* have my experiences, from which I've learned many valuable lessons that I will share with you.

I didn't perceive these lessons until I was in my early thirties. As I mentioned, I've been seeking answers since I was 12. By the time I was 16, I'd read my first psychology textbook, had learned self hypnosis and was seeing a psychiatrist. I wasn't happy with my life. In fact, I was so unhappy with who I was that I spent most of my youth hiding from myself.

When I was a boy, I was always trying to fit in. When I didn't, I became angry and sad. In fact, I tried to commit suicide a few times. I was unsuccessful because I really didn't want to die. I just wanted someone to pay attention to me. I wanted someone to hug me and tell me everything would be all right.

I felt alone even when I was surrounded by people. I was an outcast – the brunt of frequent jokes. I was also the guy who was always talked into doing things that the other kids wouldn't. Later, I became rebellious (the classic "bad boy"), and landed in jail – not once or twice, but numerous times. I was busted for everything from shoplifting to armed robbery. I was out of control. I was heading in a direction that could end only in death or a personal transformation. At the time, I would have bet money on the first outcome.

Eventually, a judge decided that enough was enough, and sentenced me to three years in prison. After 18 months, I escaped from a work camp and was free – free to get in more trouble. By this time, I should have reformed, but like most addicts, my attitude was, "I'm okay, the world's all wrong." All the promises to me, all the pledges to "wake up and smell the coffee," were quickly abandoned as I focused on surviving another day. I should have known that I was on a fast track to the cemetery, but I didn't.

I can't put my finger on a particular event that changed me forever. It was probably a combination of events. But when I think back, I *do* recall one moment.

I was sitting on the edge of a concrete slab, in solitary confinement on the 12th floor of King County Jail. Earlier in the day, I'd spoken with my attorney, who told me that there wasn't much he could do. I was going away for a few years. So that evening, I stared at the cathedral across the interstate highway. The reality of my life flooded in, and I broke down. As I stared through the barred window, I fell to my knees and begged God for forgiveness. I said, "Lord, I will do anything you ask of me. I will go to church every Sunday, and I will straighten up. I promise. Just let me out of this place. Let me go home. I'm begging you. Don't let me go to prison. I know I can change, and if you'll just give me a chance, I'll prove it. I *can* change my life and I *will*."

I prayed and I prayed, but my prayers weren't answered that night – or so I thought. The next day, I went to court, and was sentenced to three years in prison. A week later, I was placed in handcuffs and shackles, and sent "up the river."

If I had to choose a moment that marks the start of my journey toward a better self, I would pick that lonely and surreal night on the 12th floor of the county jail.

After more than 20 years of searching, during which time I've made numerous mistakes and corrections, I'm able to share what life has taught me. What I will reveal isn't especially mystical or mind blowing. Nor does it represent the latest in pop psychology – as seen in the seminars led by celebrity "gurus." Instead, this book contains a collection of tools that have helped me and hundreds of clients to become the Best Selves we can be.

Of course, even if you work the program and change your life, you won't achieve paradise on earth. You'll still encounter the same challenges and obstacles that you always have. The good news? You'll be prepared to face these challenges – to work through the chaos and drama with a positive, forward-thinking focus. You will commit to living life, and you'll never allow life to control you again.

My program is about taking control of your life. And it's all about you. It's about what you can do; right now, to change your life for the better.

I call the program "perception modification coaching," and it's composed of seven phases and 20 steps. Though my co-author and I have written what seems like a parable or a novel, the story is fact, not fiction. Only a few details were changed to protect my client's identity. In the following pages, we present a case history of how one man ("Bruce") worked the program for four months. To give you a better sense of what it's like to use the perception modification process and how to overcome certain challenges that people face along the way, we have written the tale from Bruce's point of view. It's is his real-life story.

In the next chapter, Bruce talks about what caused him to start the program. Then, we watch him work the process step by step. Once you finish the first chapter, I encourage you to work the program along with Bruce.

The key to success is a willingness to actually *work* the program. Are you ready to empower yourself and take control of your life? If not, that's okay. Maybe you'll be ready tomorrow or the next day. If you *are* ready to follow the program and take back your life – to start living instead of merely existing – then do it!

NO ORDINARY LIFE

"If you are pained by external things, it is not they that disturb you, but your own judgment of them. And it is in your power to wipe out that power now." —Marcus Aurelius

My name is Bruce, and I'm an alcoholic.

I'm many things besides an alcoholic – a husband, a homeowner, a freelance writer, a gardener and a golf enthusiast – but since problem drinking and its causes defined my life for 15 years, it's a good way to introduce myself.

If you've ever spent time at an Alcoholics Anonymous meeting, you know that every alcoholic's story is both unique *and* predictable. In other words, everyone's *drinking career* follows one of several patterns, even though the specific causes of that drinking are different. Some people seem genetically programmed for alcoholism; others aren't. Some get hooked the moment their daddies give them their first sip of beer. Others (like me) don't become full-blown alcoholics until prolonged drinking "rewires" their brains. Everyone has a different story about why and when they started drinking, but the long-term consequences of alcoholism are *always* the same – hospitals, mental wards, prisons or death.

The medical community calls alcoholism a disease, not because it resembles measles or chicken pox, but because it fits a *disease model*: it is chronic, progressive, degenerative and fatal (if left untreated). And like HIV/AIDS, you never fully recover from alcoholism. Alcoholics are always *in recovery*. We will always be *recovering* alcoholics, not *recovered* alcoholics.

I am a recovering alcoholic.

My recovery was swift and mind-blowing. I had a spiritual awakening. A new *me* suddenly occupied my body after 48 years.

It all started at gunpoint. *I* was the one holding the gun.

No, I didn't rob a liquor store.

I was a functional middle-class alcoholic. I worked my freelance business, paid my bills, rarely said an unkind word to my wife (Laura), and kept in touch with friends and family – none of whom knew the extent of my problem. Most people knew that I was a "two-fisted" drinker, but my drunkenness wasn't obvious. I didn't slur my words or stumble around. Besides, I'd been a weekend binge drinker since age 16, when I spent most Friday and Saturday nights downing cases of Molson with friends. There wasn't much for teenagers to do in Danbury, Connecticut in the '70s.

Officially, I remained a weekend social drinker until my early thirties – when my life took a dramatic turn. It began when I was fired from a New York public relations firm for "insulting" the boss. (There's more to the story, but this book isn't about office politics). From 1992 to 2002, I worked dozens of temp and permanent jobs, from bartender and word processor to legal secretary. These jobs paid the bills while I chased a new dream – becoming a film & television writer.

Landing a gig in the entertainment industry is always a long shot, but I soon discovered that I had genuine talent for creative writing, and I quickly gained plenty of education and experience. (Experience *writing* scripts, *not* being paid for them.) Despite excellent showings in nationwide contests and a few calls from literary agents, I wasn't making it in "The Industry." This weighed down my self-esteem. I was eaten away with worry that I'd never achieve my dream. I was consumed with dread every minute of every day. I was filled with regret for the paths not taken, and with remorse for my mistakes. It was only when my mind was fogged by booze that these feelings melted away – replaced by couch potato reveries in which I was being awarded Oscars for my latest screen epics.

As the months and years passed, dread morphed into defeat.

I came to believe that I'd gambled away my future on a roll of the cosmic dice, and there was no going back. There was no way to retrieve my safe and comfortable nine-to-five lifestyle. I had risked everything ... and lost. I was a loser. High-priced psychics might predict my eventual success, but they were greedy frauds. Cheerful TV actors kept telling me to follow my dreams, but they were f—king liars – corporate shills paid to keep society's drones from rebelling against their meaningless, poverty-filled lives. If only people knew how hopeless things really were – that the odds were stacked against anyone who wasn't rich or well-connected.

For a time, I behaved like a hippie. I condemned Laura as a "corporate stooge" and a "capitalist lackey" whenever she gushed about her latest career achievement or pay raise. Any success but *mine* filled me with rage. "At least once a week, Laura and I fell asleep in a tearful embrace after I poured out my fear and anger and frustrations and hopes – and then my apologies for hurting her so deeply."

She considered leaving me, but she cared too much to abandon me.

I hated myself for being a hopeless, angry drunk, but I hated everyone else even more.

My friends and relatives were lawyers and corporate managers with the words "vice president" in their job titles. They drove SUVs and lived in oversized McMansions. They were surrounded by hyperactive children, excitedly kicking the backs of airline seats when they jetted to Milan, Barbados or Bermuda on three-week vacations. And me ... well, I was trapped in a shoebox of an apartment. I had no car, no home equity, and no retirement plan. I had no future.

I was a drunken zombie – an animated corpse who was just going through the motions of living, fueled by bourbon, cigarettes and an occasional glimmer of hope. Maybe my next TV script would win recognition. Maybe I'd win a writing contest. Maybe I'd make a valuable connection by taking another screenwriting, TV writing or playwriting class, or attending another screenwriter wannabe's conference in L.A. Maybe the managing partner at the law firm where I worked would recognize my talent and promote me from secretary to the head of corporate communications, even though the firm was not a corporation and had only four lawyers.

By 1998, I had gone from weekend drinking to everyday drinking, and from wine to bourbon. If you asked me to pinpoint the moment I became a bona fide alcoholic, I couldn't do it. It was probably sometime in 1997. I was drinking a quart of bourbon every night, but would always awaken the next morning without a hangover. If I didn't have a drink by six or seven o'clock that night, however, my hands would shake, and I'd get nauseated and feverish. Occasionally, I had audio hallucinations. (I usually heard orchestras playing strange, otherworldly melodies.)

By 2002, I was an all-day drinker. I snuck bourbon to work in hip flasks, and made hourly trips to the bathroom, where a few sips of booze prevented withdrawal symptoms until lunch. Then, I'd visit any nearby tavern with a sympathetic bartender.

I was fat.
I sweated whenever I ate and or when the temperature climbed above 70.
I had frequent diarrhea.
I vomited a lot.
I smelled like whiskey-scented B.O., which is probably why my sex life fizzled like an earthworm on a hot sidewalk. For the next seven years, Laura and I didn't have sex. Whatever. My sex-drive was dead anyway.

Thanks to this unpleasantness, but mostly due to Laura's prodding – I quit drinking in the spring of 2002. Then, for six months, I visited a therapist.

I opened up to him, but I was careful *not* to blame my problems on anyone but me. My parents raised me to take responsibility for my actions – for successes *and* failures. Nobody forced me to become an alcoholic. I did this to myself. I wasn't about to blame my boozing on my parents, even though I *really* wanted to. And the idea that addiction was a disease was a cop out! That crap was for whiners and pansies. I just needed to take control of my life. But I didn't know how. Maybe the therapist knew.

He asked lots of questions, mostly about my sex life. He also advised me to join AA. I attended a meeting, but like many newcomers, I was repulsed by AA's seeming "religiosity." I had no desire to mingle with a bunch of Bible thumpers, so I fled.

I stayed sober for five months. I convinced the therapist that my drinking had been a temporary glitch caused by career insecurities. I told him that because I'd just launched a freelance business, I no longer wanted to drink every day. I told him that I could *manage* my drinking. I had retaken control of my life. Right?

Not really.

One week after I stopped seeing the therapist, I returned to my old ways. It was as if the five months of sobriety never happened ... well, almost. I soon discovered that I could no longer drink every day. By the third or fourth day of binging, I became too sick to keep drinking. Then, I'd have to endure two or three days of withdrawal symptoms before I felt "well enough" to drink again.

This became my life for the next seven years – a never-ending cycle of intoxication and detoxification. Four days of drinking were followed by three days of abstinence and flu-like symptoms. That was my schedule. I had to structure my entire life around the cycle – four days sick; three days "normal."

Need to talk with a client?
Schedule it for a "drinking day" – when I have the ability to concentrate.

A friend wants to visit on Friday?

That's a "dry day" – when I can barely function. Reschedule for the weekend.

Wife is taking a few days off work?

Hide booze in the bathroom, so she won't discover the extent of my binging.

I wasn't happy with this life, but I coped with it.

At least my career was back on track. I no longer felt like a *total* loser. I was earning money as a writer – though I'd earned *much* more as a legal secretary. On the other hand, I was proud of my status as an entrepreneur.

We moved from New York to Pennsylvania in November 2003. My father died earlier that year, leaving me enough money to buy a small house. It was a culture shock, moving from America's greatest city to a small town, but we soon embraced "country living" along a quiet cul de sac.

Unfortunately, our peace and quiet was occasionally punctuated by loud radios, foul-mouthed screaming matches and the ceaseless barking of dogs. Yep, we had one of *those* neighbors. The back of their house faced the back of ours, but it was screened by a line of cypress trees planted by the previous owner. Apparently, the last owner didn't care for these people either, and we soon learned why. None of the other neighbors had anything good to say about this family. We soon heard rumors of child beatings, drug and alcohol abuse, and accusations of break-ins and pet murders committed by the family's teenagers.

These were just rumors, but given the drunken screaming that erupted several times a month – and the never-ending barking – I believed the worst. I even bought a handgun – a .22 caliber semi-automatic. Officially, the gun was for my new target shooting hobby. In reality, I was getting anxious and angry at the noise from these "rednecks."

I was becoming even angrier than I used to be. In New York, I'd usually been happy while I was drinking. That's why I started drinking in the first place – to shut down the anger and frustration. *Now* I was getting even angrier after taking a drink. The alcohol made my problems seem even *worse*. The evening news made me angry. Politics made me angry. My meager income made me angry. My fading dreams about Hollywood made me angry. Most of all, those damned neighbors made me angry.

In July 2009, I finally "snapped." When I came home from running lunchtime errands, I was bombarded by loud music from next door. Two of the neighbors were taking a dip in their swimming pool, and (apparently) they wanted the whole neighborhood to hear their radio station. I ran inside the house, and downed a few shots of vodka. I stood in the kitchen for a moment, wondering what I should do.

Run more errands? None left.

Call the cops? No, the county had no noise ordinances.

Lose control? Great idea!

Suddenly, it felt like a stranger had taken control of my body.

I ran upstairs and grabbed the gun from its case, stuffed it in my hip pocket, bolted down the stairs, and ran around the trees to the neighbor's yard. There, I saw a middle-aged man and woman lounging in a hot tub. I approached them, waving my arms and shouting "Hello, hello!" There was no response.

I marched straight to their pool deck until I was sure they'd seen me.

"Would you turn that f—king thing down!" I shouted. "The whole f—king neighborhood can hear it!" (This request was more strongly worded than intended.)

"Who the f—k are you!" said the man.

"I'm your next-door neighbor," I replied, pointing toward my house.

"Oh, so you're the f—king a—hole who lives there!"

Now I became unhinged. Not only had this creep disturbed the peace for five years, he insulted me the moment I tried to do something about it. I yanked the gun from my pocket and thrust it in his face. "So that's the way it's gonna be, eh?"

He furrowed his brows as he squinted down the barrel of the .22. Apparently, nobody had ever responded to him this way. After several seconds, he said, "You brought a gun here? I'm calling the cops."

With those words, he turned and walked into the house.

And with those words, whatever force had taken control of my brain fled the scene. I was left standing there, shocked by my behavior and terrified of what would happen now. As the man's girlfriend (turns out he'd recently divorced) shrieked insults after me, I power-walked to my house, returned the gun to its case and hopped in my car. I might be in trouble, and didn't want to be around if the cops showed. I drove to a nearby driving range to hit a few golf balls.

When Laura got home from work, I lied. I said I'd gotten into a shouting match with the neighbor, who'd threatened to call the cops. She shook her head. "Sometimes, I just don't understand how your mind works," she said.

About 6:30 that evening, there was a knock at the front door. Laura looked up from the television and said, "Two sheriff's cars are parked in the driveway."

I opened the door, and one of two deputies asked, "Are you Bruce X?"

"Yes."

"You know why we're here, sir?"

"I can guess."

"Mr. X, I have a warrant for your arrest. Please step outside and turn around."

I did as instructed.

"Place your hands behind your back. I'm going to place handcuffs on you."

I was handcuffed as several neighbors watched from their porches. Meanwhile, the other deputy asked Laura if she'd allow him to search the house for the gun. I told him where to find it.

As Laura turned to me, I said, "I forgot to mention that there may have been a gun involved."

"I just don't understand how your mind works," she said.

The deputy escorted me to one of the waiting cars, helped me into the front passenger seat and closed the door. As we left my driveway, he read me my rights and asked if I'd be willing to tell him "what and why this happened?"

"The *what* is a long story," I replied. "The *why* is easy. I'm an alcoholic."

It was the first time I ever admitted to being an alcoholic.

To make a long story short, I was taken to the county detention center, where I was booked, given striped pants and a jersey, and placed in a holding cell with 10 other men. I spent the night there, awaiting a bond hearing in the morning. My bail was originally set at $200,000, because I was charged with multiple felonies. As luck would have it, I now lived in a county with strict gun-crime laws. Anyone caught with a handgun outside a target range or his own home was just begging for prison time.

The next morning, I was taken to a waiting area near the jail's entrance, where a group of us were placed in handcuffs, manacles and chains before being escorted to a van. On arriving at the county courthouse, we were taken to another cell to await our turns in front of a judge. When I was finally led into the courtroom, I saw Laura and my mother-in-law seated a few rows back. I was seated on a bench next to several other prisoners – some with lawyers; some forced to plead their cases alone.

As the judge was about to call my name, a gentleman in a black suit approached me. He told me that Laura had hired him as my attorney.

I have one smart wife. My new lawyer was a former Philadelphia prosecutor, and one of the best criminal defense attorneys in the area. Soon, he was arguing my case like the defense lawyers on *"Law & Order"*, telling the judge about my ties to family, the community (that was a laugh), my college education and my utter lack of a criminal record. The judge reduced the bond to $50,000.

Later that day, I was released from jail. On the drive home, Laura told me that I'd made the local news – television *and* newspapers. It must have been a slow news day. My crime was hardly front-page stuff in an area that saw dozens of assaults every week. Of course, most weren't committed by middle-aged writers.

When I walked through the front door to my house, I had my instant revelation.

It wasn't until that moment that I gained a full and complete perspective on my life. Everyday sights and sounds were now as precious as a glass of cool water to a man dying of thirst. The mundane had become the marvelous – the ordinary was extraordinary. It had finally dawned on me that I had a blessed life – a loving (and forgiving) wife, two purring cats, my own business, and my own home in the country. I had almost everything I'd always wanted – more than many people ever enjoy. And I might have thrown it all away!

What did the little annoyances *matter* now! How could I have risked all of *this* for something as trivial as loud music! I was dangerously close to losing *everything* because I hadn't controlled my temper – because I was addicted to a chemical that impaired my judgment and unleashed my irrational impulses.

I was suddenly in love with my life!

In the following weeks, I entered an outpatient rehab facility and joined Alcoholics Anonymous. In both places, I learned more about alcohol and substance abuse than the average person will ever know. More important, I learned that the overwhelming majority of people who kick the habit undergo spiritual transformations like the one I'd had. Counseling and abstinence takes you only so far. To succeed, you must *rebuild your life* on a solid foundation. You must change your perspective and your perceptions. You must understand that it's not outer circumstances that determine whether you will be happy, but the quality of your mind. How you perceive the world dictates how you react to the world. Your perceptions determine whether you will thrive or suffer. I learned these lessons – and more – by reviewing my own experiences and those of my fellow addicts.

Unfortunately, one big question remained: How could I *permanently* alter my inner life? How could I be sure that my outer circumstances would never again overwhelm my inner peace and gratitude? Could anyone guide me on my journey to happiness and fulfillment? Was long-term happiness even possible?

PHASE 1: WHERE ARE YOU TODAY?

The Master observes the world, but trusts his inner vision. He allows things to come and go. His heart is as open as the sky."—Lao-tzu

I was introduced to Dr. Lieber through my addiction counselor at Stillwater Recovery, which was housed in a Victorian mansion that had seen better days. I was enrolled in a 26-week outpatient program that featured 3-times-a-week group therapy/drug & alcohol education sessions, as well as one-on-one meetings with my counselor, Lindsay. She was a sassy 25-year-old who masked her empathy with a sarcastic "drill sergeant" persona.

We were in her office one afternoon, discussing my odds of avoiding prison, when I told her that I was almost happy about my legal mess. If the universe, the Tao, God – whatever governed the cosmos – hadn't brought me to this point, I might have suffered a worse fate. But now, I was filled with gratitude and a serenity that enhanced my perceptions of life. I wondered, however, if these feelings were just "the pink cloud" phenomenon – a temporary euphoria that some recovering addicts experience. I worried that my new perspective would suddenly vanish. I wondered how I could hold on to my mental and spiritual gains.

Lindsey asked if I'd ever heard of perception modification. I hadn't, but the term conjured images of *A Clockwork Orange* – where the protagonist is strapped to a chair with his eyelids clamped open, forced to watch violent films until the mere thought of violence makes him physically ill.

"That was sci-fi *behavioral* modification," said Lindsey. "Perception modification is a process that helps people achieve their goals by changing the way they perceive the past and present. You work with a coach who helps you analyze your past experiences – especially traumatic memories – to figure out how they shaped your outlook. Then you learn how to modify your perceptions to become a happier person. There aren't any experimental drugs or torture devices. It's more like a combination of therapy and life coaching."

She began typing on her computer keyboard. "Here we go."

She hit a final key and walked to a nearby printer. A single sheet of paper emerged, and she handed it to me.

"I met Dr. Lieber a few years ago. He gave a presentation about his program. He doesn't treat addictions or mental illnesses. That's *my* job. But his perception modification process can help you uncover the causes of your addiction and learn how to deal with them."

"Is he taking new patients?"

She shrugged. "Call and find out."

"Okay. I just hope we don't have to conduct our sessions in prison."

"He lives in Idaho – too far away for prison visits."

"What a relief."

"Besides, you're not going to prison. County jail, maybe."

Dr. Lieber was working with a client when I called later that day, but he returned my call within an hour. I gave him a *Reader's Digest* condensed version of my life, focusing mainly on my boozing and the career problems that fueled it. I also mentioned Lindsey's referral and her brief description of his program.

He said the perception modification process was inspired by key concepts and practices drawn from (and sometimes shared by) modern psychology, life coaching and the philosophies of Taoism and Buddhism. The process was designed to promote optimal health in all four areas of life – physical, mental, emotional and spiritual – by helping clients achieve their *Best Selves*, however they define that.

The process is based on the notion that people *are* the sum total of their experiences. Because experiences define us, they can either block progress toward mental, emotional, physical and spiritual well-being, or highlight the paths to optimal health. Wellness hinges on our *perception* of our experiences and the *positive* lessons we draw from them.

Behavior is taught through how we perceive events and experiences. Some of these experiences may be positive and joyful. For example, when we do well at our jobs we may receive a compliment or a pay raise. A positive action yields a positive reaction by prompting us to do the best we can. On the other hand, some experiences produce negative reactions. For instance, a middle child may feel she isn't getting enough attention and act out, causing her parents to react with stern discipline. The child learns that bad behavior generates the attention she craves (albeit negative attention). Over time, this lesson is reinforced again and again, clouding the child's perceptions and behavior into adulthood.

Our perception often becomes skewed, especially if we weren't privy to all the information surrounding the original experiences. As time goes by, we may even repress the experiences because of the associated trauma, never realizing that these experiences greatly influenced who we became. As a result, we may have overlooked valuable life lessons and hidden gifts. People who always fall short of accomplishing their goals may be suffering from skewed perceptions triggered by events that are long past and long forgotten. This is where the perception modification process can help.

The perception modification process consists of *Seven Steps*:

1. Where Are You Today?
2. Discovering Your Best Self.
3. Identifying Obstacles, Challenges and Strategies.
4. Rediscovering Your Past.
5. Planning and Goal Setting.
6. Initiating Your Plan.
7. Maintaining Optimal Wellness.

"This program is unlike any other you may have encountered," said Dr. Lieber. "It doesn't involve counseling, and it isn't meant to point out your faults. It's designed to help you identify your positive qualities, and use them to achieve your Best Self.

"The first phase is identifying who you are today. This step is the foundation of the program. It allows us to identify where our starting point is. This step isn't meant to confirm all of the bad things in your life. It's meant to help us establish a baseline.

"The second phase is equally important. This is the vision phase. It lets us open up our imagination, and create a vision of who we want to become. There are no limits or boundaries in this phase. We let our imaginations roam freely. The vision of who you want to become is what we will work to achieve. During this phase, we consider all four aspects of our lives – our physical being, our mental and emotional health and finally, our spiritual health. We want to consider our whole being, not just one or two aspects.

"For example, maybe we'll decide that you're a little overweight – that you're an emotional eater. To realize your Best Self vision, you want to lose weight and overcome the causes of emotional eating.

"The next phase is often considered the most difficult. This is the discovery phase. Here, we look at your past experiences, and revisit certain events that you've endured – events with a direct or indirect impact on you today. I want to stress, however, that we do *not* relive those experiences. We simply revisit them. When we identify events that have affected who you are today, we sift through each one to determine if we can modify how you perceive it. Our goal is to transform each experience from a negative to a positive.

"The key is changing how we perceive the experiences, and discovering if there are any useful lessons that will support us in achieving our Best Self. You'd be surprised how often we take past experiences and use them to help us accomplish our goals.

"The fourth phase is about goal-setting. Most people know how to set goals, so this phase is usually quick. We learn the steps used to set goals – positive and achievable goals – that we'll implement in phase five.

"In phase five, we plan strategies to achieve the goals. We take the daily steps, which we planned earlier, to reach our short-term, mid-term and long-term goals.

"The sixth phase is the revisiting phase. We revisit our initial vision and goals and if necessary, we modify them. As we move forward, our lives change. Even in the short period from phase one to phase six, our lives may change enough to require an adjustment to the original vision and goals. For instance, if your original goal was to lose 20 pounds and you lost the 20 pounds in three months, you'll need a new goal. So, your new vision may be to maintain your current weight, and your new goal will be consistently eating right.

"The seventh phase is the maintenance phase – maintaining our vision once we achieve it, and changing it when necessary. Life changes and we must be willing to change with it. When life throws us a curveball, we don't panic or let chaos control us. We use the tools we've acquired to help control how we deal with life. The best part of this program is that once you've successfully completed all seven phases, you'll have the tools needed to deal with most of life's challenges.

"Basically, the program is set up to help you become independent and empowered and to put me out of business.

"So what do you think so far?"

I didn't know what to think. Creating a Best Self? Goal-setting? It sounded like some bullshit self-help seminar. Next thing you know, Dr. Lieber would have me chanting affirmations into a mirror – "I am a strong and self-actualized man who can achieve all his goals, blah, blah, blah." This is the sort of New Age rubbish that comedy writers make fun of. On the other hand … revisiting past experiences to understand their impact on my life today? Well, that *might* be interesting.

"Do you think the program would work for you?" he asked.

"It sounds interesting," I said. "I'm just not sure it's a good fit. I'm pretty self-aware, as most writers are, so I don't need someone to pinpoint the sources of my problems. I know where I am and how I got here. Aside from excessive drinking, I don't really have many problems. This program sounds like it was meant for people who are *really* screwed up."

"Bruce, the program is flexible. It's designed to help people with *any* challenges, major or minor. You don't have to be screwed up to achieve your Best Self. The program is tailored to *your* visions and *your* goals. It's not a one-size-fits-all approach. If we go through the vision phase, and you discover only one thing you want to change, then we'll work on just that one thing."

"I also want to stress that this program is only meant to provide you with tools that can help you develop your 'best you.' If you're almost there, great, that just means we'll move through the program even faster. The bottom line is, if you feel that the program could benefit you, let's proceed. If you feel that it has nothing to offer, then that's fine, too. The program is meant to guide you toward empowerment – toward taking back your life. But it's not my job to tell you what to do. It's my job to provide you with options, and right now you have two options: start the program or don't."

I thought for a moment before saying, "Let me get back to you."

As I hung up, I heard the front door open and close. I caught a glimpse of Laura disappearing up the stairs.

"Hey babe, how was work?" I called.

"Same old, same old," said Laura. "How was yours?"

"It could have been worse. I called that doctor today."

"And …"

"He went over his program with me. I don't know if it's for me."

"What do you mean?" She appeared at the entrance to my office, wearing a T-shirt and jeans. "What don't you like about the program?"

19

"It's for people whose lives are total wrecks. My only challenges today are staying off booze and out of prison. The doc's program is meant for people who've lost their jobs and homes because they're drug addicts or emotional cripples."

At that instant, I knew I'd stuffed my foot in my mouth. I saw a look in Laura's eyes that I'd never seen in all the years I'd known her. Her eyes were squinted, her lips pulled close together and her complexion had turned gray. She began to tremble.

"How dare you— You think everything's fine?" she stammered. You must be blind! Has this entire experience been in vain? I can't believe you think everything is okay because you promised, for the zillionth time, to stop drinking!"

"It's not just a promise this—"

"Yes it is! It's another empty promise until you commit to turning your life around. Rehab is a good start, but once that's finished, most alcoholics crawl back into the bottle. You need something *more* to make sure that doesn't happen. You *need* this program. You at least *need* to give it a try!

"Have you looked in the mirror lately? Don't you realize what your behavior has done to you – what it's done to *us*? Do you really think our lives are perfect, except for a few hiccups? I just spent $10,000 on attorney's fees – money I didn't have. I pledged all the equity in our house to bail you out. Did you ever stop to think about that? And if our lawyer can't keep you out of prison, I'll be stuck here paying the mortgage and the bills without you. Hey, no problem, right? As long as you promise to stay away from alcohol, everything is cool!"

She stormed up the stairs, slamming the bedroom door.

I stood in my office – my head spinning. Laura had never talked to me like that. It wasn't her nature to be harsh.

I'd pressed her to the brink of emotional collapse. I'd pressed our marriage to the brink of collapse. There was only one solution if I hoped to save our relationship. I needed to commit to Dr. Lieber and commit *now*. I had to work the program and make it work for me. I had to do it for Laura, for our marriage and for myself.

Session #1:

"Bruce, you aren't alone on your journey to understanding who you are and why you arrived at this crossroads in your life," said Dr. Lieber. "Most people have stood – or will someday stand – where you are today. The key difference is that *you* are taking the first steps toward self-discovery."

"Too bad I didn't take those steps 30 years ago," I said.

"At least you're on the path. The vast majority of the world's people will never understand themselves. Let me ask you this: Have you ever seen a homeless person?"

"I'm a former New Yorker."

"So you've seen people curled up in alleys, looking cold and hungry. And you're no stranger to addiction yourself. So when you see a homeless person, do you ever ask, 'How in the world did he end up like that? Was he once a father, a husband or the CEO of a large corporation? What went wrong? Did he get hooked on drugs? Was he raised in an abusive household? Did he drop out of school and have run-ins with the law?'"

"I've asked those questions."

"And today you're asking, 'How did *I* reach this point? Why has my life turned out like *this?*'"

"Yes."

"Life is confusing and frustrating, and we sometimes lose our way. You're asking profound questions, and you want answers. I've spent my life looking for the answers. From my earliest years, I wasn't satisfied or happy with the person staring back at me from the mirror. Time and again, I was told I needed to change, or I'd end up in jail or dead. Unfortunately, even though everyone saw that my behavior was reckless, nobody could show me how to change. They couldn't help, because they couldn't offer me tools to reshape my life. All they knew was that I was heading in the wrong direction.

"After thousands of hours of research and analysis, I transformed my seemingly negative experiences into a perception modification process that can help anyone find solutions to life's biggest challenges. It's a process that puts you squarely on the path to improving your life and your future. There's no mystery to the process, no gimmicks and (unfortunately) no guarantees. Positive results depend on your willingness and readiness to change your life and follow the process to its conclusion.

"So before we go any further, I'm going to email you *Seven Key Questions*. Take a few hours or a few days to mull them over, and give me a call."

"I can probably answer them right now – if you have time."

"Are you near a computer? You should have the email by now."

I was already sitting at my desk, so I grabbed my mouse and opened the email.

I didn't need days to answer these questions. I immediately asked and answered every question aloud:

1. *"Is life working for you?* Not entirely.
2. *"Are you happy right now?* Same answer.
3. *"Are you being honest with yourself?* Yes.
4. *"If you were to continue in your current direction – if everything stayed the same – would you feel satisfied and complete a year from now, two years from now, five years from now?* No.
5. *"Do you constantly think that there's more to life than you currently have?* Yes.
6. *"If you've already tried other self-help programs, therapy, etc., are you willing to try a different approach to improving your life?* Yes.
7. *"If you're dissatisfied and ready to make a change – are you willing to surrender to life and let yourself receive?* Yes. But I'm not sure what you mean by 'surrendering to life.' "

"You are surrendering your ego and accepting what life has to offer," said Dr. Lieber. Even if you're *willing* to make change, you may not be *ready*.

"One of my clients' biggest challenges is letting go of the ego complex – getting past the 'me' syndrome. If you want to promote your ego through this process, it won't be effective. The process is much more likely to work when you say, 'This is where I am, and I'm not happy. There's more to life. I want to reach the next level, and I'm willing to do what it takes.'

"Begin with an empty vessel – empty your mind, your soul and your heart. Empty out all the trash and say, 'I know this will be difficult. I know it's going to be challenging. I know it's going to be new. I have no idea where I'm going, but I will trust that where I'm going is *where I want to go*. That's an essential step.

"Everyone's life is filled with possibilities. There are no limitations in life other than the ones we create. You can make excuses such as 'I grew up in a dysfunctional family' or 'we were dirt poor,' but those are just excuses. You can accomplish anything you want. It's up to you. It depends on what you foresee as your Best Self.

"Are you *really* ready for change? The majority of people seeking deeper self-awareness are not. Many people read self-help books and attend seminars because they're unhappy. They don't like their current situations. But this doesn't mean they're actually ready for change.

"Alcoholics can lose their family, their jobs – they can lose everything – and still refuse to make changes. They *know* that the path they're on isn't good: it's full of pain and heartache. But when you sit them down

PRESS THE "FIX ME" BUTTON

and say, 'Here's an opportunity to enter rehab and improve your life,' most will continue to drink. They fall back on alcohol rather than seizing the opportunity."

"I know *that* path all too well," I said.

"I'm sure you do. So does my brother. He's a great guy, but alcohol has cost him his wife and his children. Instead of focusing on how to create a better life, he chooses to live in the 'ditches of chaos.' In part, this is because he doesn't know where to go and how to change. He's also comfortable with the lifestyle of an alcoholic, making it even more difficult to change.

"We're discussing Phase #1 right now: *Where Are You Today?* This phase is critical, so ask yourself, 'Am I ready?' No excuses. You'll only be making excuses to yourself. Are there things you really want to change in your life? Are you ready to do what it takes, or are you going to do this for a month, and make excuses about why you can't continue. Don't tell me, 'Yeah, yeah, let's get on with it' if you aren't ready to really commit to change.' I hate wasting my time."

"I don't blame you," I said.

"We make these half-hearted commitments with our New Year's resolutions, right? We resolve that we're going to launch these terrific diets, eat healthy, quit smoking, quit drinking, quit this and that. We abide by our resolutions for a few days, and then backslide into our old habits. Why? Because we aren't *truly* committed to making those changes!

"You must also accept that this process won't produce results overnight. Like anything else in life, you won't wake up one morning and have all the answers. You're like a toddler learning to walk. You're going to fall. We call that 'error and correction.' We fall, we get up and we correct ourselves. We continue falling, getting up, evaluating our mistakes, and correcting those mistakes until walking becomes natural and habitual.

"It's a process. And it doesn't happen overnight.

"One thing that distinguishes my process from therapy is that I am *not* your therapist – I'm your coach. I'm not going to label the causes of your unhappiness or anxiety, and then try to alleviate the symptoms. We *will* identify the causes of your unhappiness, anxiety, self-defeating behavior and so on, but once we do, we will apply *forward thinking* methods to help you achieve your goals and dreams. Yes, we will examine some of the events that brought you to this point. But we won't *relive* them. I strenuously encourage my clients to avoid reliving events and re-experiencing the emotions that caused them so much suffering in the past.

23

"In addition, I should stress that *this is your program.* I'm the coach on the sidelines; you're the player on the field. It's like playing soccer. I'm not out there kicking the ball. You're out there kicking the ball. But I have something you don't. I have the ability to see the whole game unfolding on the field while you're focusing on where the ball is. I'll coach you from the sidelines as you focus on achieving your Best Self. I'll throw you into the game at different times with different 'game plays.' These game plays are the various tools and exercises we use to accomplish your goals.

"Unlike therapy, my opinion doesn't matter. I'm not going to insert my opinions into the process, because the process is all about you and your opinions. You figure it out. I'll *help* you figure it out, but in the end, *you* control the process.

"Believe it or not, you are exactly where you were meant to be – right now. According to the Tao, we are always where we were meant to be at any given moment. You've been led to this place to change your life for the better. So was I. You were brought here so that you could climb from a pit of despair. I was brought here to help."

"That's very altruistic of you," I said.

"Yes and no. Serving others is both selfless *and* selfish. Serving causes greater than ourselves is the surest way to acquire lasting happiness and contentment. If we serve only our own needs and desires – especially when we chase after material possessions and ego-boosting achievements – we'll find ourselves on a treadmill. Psychologists call this the 'hedonic treadmill.' The more possessions and achievements we gain, the more of them we need just to stay in place. Does that make sense?"

"Perfect sense," I replied.

"If you believe your life is crap, guess what? Your life is crap. When you choose to no longer live a crappy life, you take an important step. The first step out of crap is acknowledging that you're living in it and that you don't want to live there anymore. The perception modification process helps you build a ladder to get out of the crap. All you need to do is commit to building and using the ladder.

"Do you have any questions?"

"I probably will. Right now, I'm still digesting everything. I can tell you this much, though. I am *really* ready to get started."

"I'm *really* happy to hear that. How does next Friday look? I have an opening at … two o'clock your time."

"Two o'clock is great."

"Wonderful. Before then, I'm going to give you some homework – your first exercise. I want you to list one thing you'd like to change in each of the four areas of health – physical, mental, emotional and spiritual. Write one or two sentences about something you'd like to change in each area. These are your objectives. For example, in the physical realm, you might want to drop a few pounds. And in the mental arena, you might want to banish foggy thinking. And so on.

"Then, next to each objective, list your 'motivators' – some reasons why you want to make the change. Identify which reasons are based on fear, which are based on rewards or both. Finally, list any challenges you might encounter when trying to make these changes, and determine how you'll overcome the challenges."

"No problem," I said.

"Remember, keep it short. You don't have to write a novel."

"Can do."

"I usually have clients do this exercise after Session #1 – not after the initial consultation – but since you've answered the 7 Key Questions and I've learned where you are today, I'd say we've finished the first session. What do you think?"

"I think I'm ready to roll, doc."

PHASE 2:
DISCOVERING YOUR BEST SELF

"We are formed and molded by our thoughts. Those whose minds are shaped by selfless thoughts give joy when they speak or act." —The Buddha

Session #2:

After hanging up with Dr. Lieber, I sat down at my computer to write my change statements. I was excited about the exercise, and wanted to capture my thoughts while our conversation was still fresh in my mind. As soon as I finished, I attached the document to an email for the doc, and shot it into cyberspace.

Changes I'd Like to Make	
<u>Physical:</u>	To lose weight.
<u>Mental:</u>	To be more creative in my thinking.
<u>Emotional:</u>	To better control any feelings of fear and anger.
<u>Spiritual:</u>	To develop the ability to consciously connect with the divine.

Fifteen minutes later, I got a reply from Dr. Lieber. Because I was expecting a pat on the back for my brilliant insights, I was disappointed with his message. It seems I'd botched my first homework assignment.

Re: Vision Statement
Date: 11/20/2009
From: dr.lieber@hitmail.com
To: gr&twriter@aul.com

Hi Bruce,
    Thanks for sending me the exercise so quickly.
    Well, you're off to a good start! The change statements about the emotional and spiritual components of your life are right on target. However, you forgot to include your Motivators and Challenges for all 4 components. In addition, the statements about your physical and mental life are too vague. Don't worry. This is a problem many of my clients have when tackling this exercise for the first time. In fact, you're one step ahead of the crowd, since you nailed two of them right off the bat!
    The problem with the physical and mental statements is that, while you identified problems you want to solve, you didn't translate those problems into positive outcomes. One purpose of change statements is to transform negatives into positives by stating the *goal* you will achieve. For example, many people say, "I want to lose weight" or "I want to run faster." This is typical of how most people think.
    What I want *you* to do is to make your goal the "main attraction" of each statement.
    If you want to lose weight, decide on your ideal weight, and write that into your statement. "I will reach my ideal weight of 175 pounds." If you want to be more creative in your thinking, you might say, "I will better identify my clients' problems, and propose strategies that solve those problems." These statements are more specific and goal-oriented.
    I hope this helps. Take another swing at the exercise, and call me if you have any difficulties.
    Dr. Lieber

The moment I finished reading the email, a veil was lifted from my eyes. I felt like an idiot, because I now knew *exactly* what to write. An hour later, I emailed my revised list, which included my reasons for wanting to make the changes and the challenges confronting me.

Changes I'd Like to Make

Physical: To reach my ideal weight by losing (roughly) 20 to 30 pounds. *Motivators:* to look better, feel more energetic, and reduce the likelihood of certain injuries and illnesses. (The first two motivators are reward-based; the rest are fear-based.) *Challenges:* I tend to eat large portions and I LOVE snacking.

Mental: To think in more innovative ways, especially in terms of growing my business. *Motivators:* to increase the quality of my work, attract more clients and raise my income. (All of these motivators are reward-based.) *Challenges:* It's easier to stick to routines – to be lazy.

Emotional: To better control feelings of fear and anger. *Motivator:* to prevent episodes like the one that landed me in "hot water." (Fear-based motivator.) *Challenges:* Negative emotions often sneak up on me before I recognize them.

Spiritual: Develop the ability to consciously connect with the divine. *Motivator:* to discover answers to life's problems and increase my overall happiness. (One motivator is fear-based; the other reward-based.) *Challenges:* Eventually, I grow doubtful of anything that cannot be detected with the five senses.

When Dr. Lieber answered the phone the following week, his first words were: "Bruce! What wonderful things have happened to since we last spoke?"

I soon discovered that he opened every session with these words. I also learned that this wasn't some trademarked greeting. He *really* wanted to know about the wonderful things that had happened. If I couldn't think of anything, we'd review the previous week's events until he identified an event he could positively "spin."

During the previous week, for example, a local contractor came to replace our septic system. Since the price tag was nearly $10,000, I wasn't thrilled. Worse: on the day the workmen arrived to tear up my yard, our region was smacked by a snowstorm. As the workers were packing up their tools that afternoon, one of them accidentally turned off our water pump. (We didn't know this until days later.) By the time I discovered that we were without water, the workers were long gone. A call to their office was met with speculation that they might have severed the water main. However, there was nothing they could do until after the storm. I scrambled to find a plumber willing to drive through the blizzard. When I found one, he charged me $150 to rig a hose from my neighbor's outdoor spigot to my house. At least we had running water for the next three days.

"Well, I *did* take everything in stride while Laura was freaking out. She kept imagining worst-case scenarios: 'What if the water pump is still running, gets overheated and sets the house on fire?' Things like that."

"You were her backbone – her support team."

"Yes."

"In some respects, the situation allowed you to give her the physical, mental and emotional support that she needed at the time. Also, by affirming the need to live in the moment and to stop thinking in terms of worst case scenarios, maybe a little green light will soon flash in her mind, and she'll say, 'Oh, I get it! I don't have to live in constant fear of what *might* happen.'

"Anyway, I've reviewed your homework, and it looks like you've been able to identify areas to improve that will give you solid direction. I'd suggest that you buy a three-ring binder, so you can organize all your written exercises, and keep the printed sheets in one place for easy reference. It's nice to have everything organized so you can reflect back to where you began – compared to where you will be later."

"No problem. I have a load of extra binders for my biz."

"Good. Now let's talk about your Best Self vision. Briefly, what we're going to do – and this will be part of your homework for next week – is discuss what the Best Self is and the Best Self *Vision*. Now that we've talked about where you are and identified things you'd like to change, we want to look at your very Best Self. We're going to do a forward projection.

"If you close your eyes and envision *you* at your very best, what do you see? Where do you see yourself – physically, mentally, emotionally and spiritually? When I close *my* eyes, I see myself on the West Coast at a nice little beach house. I'm running through the sand in the morning with my grandchildren, or walking along the shore with my wife. I'm physically strong and healthy. Go through this process in your mind's eye.

"What we want to do is create a Vision Statement. Now, a vision statement is not an explanation. It should start with 'I am …' and then address every area of your health. For example, a vision statement might start with 'I am … at my ideal weight … I am able to think outside the box. I am emotionally secure with myself,' etc.

"We need to know where we're going. We need a blueprint for the Best Self that we are going to build. It needs to be a *confirmed* statement – not 'I would *like* to be,' but 'I *am*. I *am* 30 pounds lighter.' How's your physical health and appearance? How's your mental health? How's your emotional health? Are you on a beach, playing with your children in the sand, running effortlessly without losing your breath? Is every day filled with joy and gratitude and appreciation? Are you excited? The vision statement can incorporate all these things. It's how you see yourself at your very best, and it's going to be essential for us in moving forward.

"Sit down and write a vision statement. Typically, it's no more than five or ten sentences. It's very specific. It's very blunt. It's very short. It's not a lengthy explanation. Once it's done, we will work on transforming the vision statement into a Vision Pictorial – a short story. But that's for later.

"Next week, write your vision statement. What this does for you and me – since I don't know you backwards and forwards – is determine what we're working *toward*. Then, if you run into a challenge or an obstacle along the way, I can help you develop options to move through those challenges, because I'll know what we're moving toward. The vision statement also gives you a good idea of where you want to go. Many times, we don't give much thought to where we want to go. We simply wish we could do this or that. That gives you plenty of great ideas, but no clear sense of direction.

"I also want you to start a Vision Board. A vision board is a confirmation. As you assemble it, it will give you a daily confirmation of your vision. If you believe that you've *already* acquired what you want, and you *confirm* it, then you *will* acquire it. If you believe that you *might* be able to do this or that, and you're not sure or don't really believe what you're saying, you probably won't put much effort into achieving the goal. That's why it's important to have that vision board right in front of you.

"Don't start chopping up and pasting a million magazines as if you were composing a collage or a ransom note. Just buy a 2' x 4' poster board, and put it where you'll be forced to see it everyday – where you'll be forced to confirm what you're working toward. I always find this part of the process a lot of fun. It's part of the discovery process, which is very exciting. It's adventurous. It's all about what you want – whether they are material things or more abstract things.

"If you want a family – and you come across a picture of a harmonious family in a magazine – cut out that picture and paste it to your vision board. If you're flipping through a magazine and see a picture of your 'dream house,' cut out the picture and put it on your vision board.

"There are no limitations to the vision board. Put anything and everything on there. You don't do it overnight. It's done over time. You certainly *can* sit down and start cutting out a bunch of pictures if you want, as long as what you put on the board is what you want in life.

I said, "But they don't *have* to be photographs, right? I assume you could also draw—"

"Absolutely," said Dr. Lieber. "It's your board."

"Okay."

"You can draw pictures, clip photos, take photos yourself, and paint—"

I said, "I know what you mean. I saw somebody creating a sort of vision board on TV – on a home and garden program. They wanted to create a new landscape around their home, with flowers, ponds, etc, and that's exactly what they did. They pasted all these magazine photos of landscapes on a board."

"That's exactly what we want – a rough blueprint of your Best Self," said Dr. Lieber. Discovering your Best Self is like building a house. A builder can't build a house without knowing what he wants to construct. Right now, you may not know *exactly* what you want to build, but you have to have some vision – how many windows, how many doors, and how many floors do you anticipate? Does the house have a front porch? Where is it located?

"The next part of the process will be drafting a more detailed blueprint, which is the Vision Pictorial. It's more defined. I tell clients that I want to close my eyes and envision exactly what *they* see by looking at their Vision Boards. This is important. I need to know what you *want* in order to coach you toward these goals.

"Keep in mind that your Best Self *will* change. The discovery process is not static, because *you* are not static. As you grow, the Best Self will grow, too. What we see as our Best Self today may not be what we'll see as our Best Self down the road. What we're learning now is how to gather the right tools and how to use them.

"For example, if you remember when you were in your twenties—"

"I think I can," I laughed.

"Remember what life was like for you. You were young. You may have been in college, having fun with your friends and girlfriends. Things were much different back then. Now move ahead to midlife. Let's look where we are halfway through life. Things that were important when we were in our twenties seem trivial today. We look back and think, 'That was foolish' because those concerns are no longer important."

"Right!"

"So this is *today's* Best Self that we're identifying. Three months from now, when we go back through the process of rewriting the vision statement, I guarantee that it will be different, because your views and how you perceive your life will be different.

"Does this make sense?"

"I think I see where you're going, but—"

"But ..."

"I ... this seems like standard-issue self-help stuff. No disrespect, but vision boards and statements? I'm supposed to look at a board and a statement and say, 'I'm already there! I already have these things!' The reality is that I don't. Is this part of the process – fooling myself into thinking that I already have all of these great things?"

"You aren't trying to fool yourself. You're developing a knowledge of what you will attain – a vision so powerful and clear that it's *almost* as if you're there already. We're still in the earliest stages of the process. You haven't fully surrendered to it yet. You haven't become the empty vessel."

"I'm not sure how to *be* an empty vessel," I said.

"I'll give you an example.

"Growing up, I had a close friend who became a drug addict. She was into a lot of hardcore stuff – like cocaine and methamphetamine. When she became pregnant with a daughter, however, she started cleaning herself up. Unfortunately, when the daughter was a few years old, she was killed while playing behind a parked car. The driver didn't see the girl, and backed over her.

"At that moment, my friend had to make a decision. She could easily have gone back to her addictions, which most people would have done, or she could find the strength to forward focus. She chose the second path. Rather than falling back into substance abuse, she chose to seek help and seek out answers in life. Today, she speaks at AA and NA events around the country to share her story and her strength."

"I like to tell this story because my friend was a substance abuser who grew up in a very dysfunctional environment. Despite this – and despite

33

the loss of her daughter – she always understood that she had choices. No matter how difficult life seemed, she *knew* she had to surrender to the process of her life. She had to surrender her heart, her soul, and every ounce of her being without any idea of where she was going – without any idea of what would happen next or how to deal with it.

"It's a scary process, but life has a lot to offer if you allow it. Most people restrict themselves because they won't let go of the belief that they're in full control of their lives. This is a false sense of control, and when you recognize that, surrendering becomes easier. The idea that we can fully control our lives is a perception we must modify."

"*Now* I see where we're going!" I said.

Dr. Lieber added, "Through the perception modification process, we will evaluate the key experiences that brought you to this point in your life – not relive them, but evaluate them.

"First, we have to know where you are today and where you want to go. You must work to release your ego's fear of 'losing control' because the ego is never in control in the first place. As long as your ego resists what life has to offer, you are like the kayaker who insists on paddling upstream against a mighty waterfall. You may succeed in making *some* progress, but you're unlikely to achieve many of your dearest goals. And what little progress you make will come at the expense of ceaseless and exhausting struggle.

"My friend could have filled herself with blame and fear, hate and anger. That would be a typical response to such a tragedy. Instead, she said, 'What is hidden in this event? What life lessons are hidden here? What gifts have I acquired from this experience that I can pass forward to other people?'

"When you view something as a gift and not a tragedy, you understand that sometimes you acquire precious insights and personal growth from adversity. You stop playing it safe. You learn to take risks because you're no longer terrified of what lies around the next corner.

"Another reason for the vision statement and (later) the vision pictorial has to do with a concept put forth in *The Secret*.

"I've heard of the book," I said.

"It's not a new concept," said Dr. Lieber, "but it was well presented. The 'secret' is merely this: when you believe something already exists, you will attract it to you. If you believe you live in a world of negativity, you will attract negativity. If you believe you live in a positive world, you will attract positive things. You will attract into your life what you feel is already in your life. That's a very important concept.

"Let's say there are two kids growing up in the same neighborhood. They went to the same schools and both came from underprivileged backgrounds. Today, one is a lawyer living in high-rise condo in New York while the other lives in a trailer in the ghetto. Why the difference? Well, the trailer guy probably makes all sorts of excuses, but the bottom line is that the other guy believed he was a lawyer living in a New York high-rise. He believed *that* was his life. He chose to extract himself from a negative lifestyle. He said, 'I'm a lawyer. I'm going to live in New York City. I'm going to have my own condo.' Those thoughts guided the actions that *brought* these things into his life. That's what he believed, so that's what materialized.

"It's easy to get trapped in the world of 'I can't.' The first step to discovering who you are is to say, 'You know what? I've lived my whole life in a negative world, but now I'm going to move forward and make some changes.'

"This is why I introduce the vision board into the process. I tell clients to make sure the vision board is in a high-traffic location, so they see it every day. They should put it on the bathroom mirror, next to their bed or wherever, but I want them to look at that board every day. And rather than thinking, 'These are the things I wish for,' I tell clients to say, 'These *are* the things in my life.'"

"That makes sense," I said.

"Good. Just one other thing before we finish our session.

"I want to reemphasize that this is your story. This is your journey. You must decide that the only way to change your life is by changing yourself. No one else can do it for you. You need to say, 'I am not going to rely on my husband and my children to follow this diet. I'm *going* to follow this diet. If they chose to come along with me, cool. If they choose not to, fine. I am in *my* journey. I'm going to focus on my business and what *I* want to do with life.'

"*That* is very self-empowering. You're taking back control. Again, you can't fully control every aspect of your life – things happen – but you can take the rudder of your boat and steer toward a specific point along the shore. If you want to quit smoking, tell yourself, 'I'm going to quit.' And you quit. If you like to smoke, then tell yourself, 'I like to smoke and that's what I'm going to do.' Make your own choices.

"The perception modification process is not a blame game. I'm not here to reinforce your perception that you mother or father did something that justifies your behavior. I'm not here to pinpoint excuses. The process demands that you stay in your own business and keep others out of your business.

"It boils down to boundaries.

"I'll discuss boundaries in more detail as we move to the later steps, but here's a quick summary: We must establish boundaries in our lives regarding things that are acceptable and things that are not acceptable. Many times, we choose to live outside of our personal boundaries. I call that 'living in somebody else's business.' We often live in other people's business. You see this with people who like to gossip. They're gossiping because they're always living in everybody else's business.

"It occurred to me that the reason they're living in other people's business is because the more they live there, the less they have to live in their *own* business. They're insecure with themselves. They're insecure with their lives. They're not happy. They don't want to focus on *their* lives, so they focus on other people's lives."

"That explains the entire gossip magazine industry," I said.

"It does," he laughed.

I added, "If this process is as good as advertised, you'll put *People* magazine out of business."

"If you think about it, that's what most people thrive on – the problems of other people. They are living in other people's business. They don't want to reflect on themselves, because when they do, they're scared to death. Suddenly, all of these insecurities bubble up, and they freak out.

"I'm working on boundaries with one of my clients. She's doing a terrific job, but she's still very insecure. She's afraid of standing up for herself. She's an older woman whose been made to feel insecure much of her life.

"I've been helping her stay in her business. One day, a coworker – someone who behaves like she's the boss but isn't – asked her, 'Did you lock everything up last night?' And my client said, 'Yes.' Then the other woman said, 'Did you shut off all the lights?' My client said, 'I already told you that I shut everything off.' The other woman responded, 'Did you lock the doors?' And my client said, 'I already told you.' Finally, as the other woman was saying 'did you ...' my client looked her in the eyes and said, 'I told you the first time, so there's no reason to continue asking me.' The other woman walked away.

"Well, this individual went back to her office and worked herself up into a frantic cry. About a half-hour later, she stormed out of the office and didn't return for the rest of the day. My client was really upset, so I asked her, 'Do you know for certain that she left because of you? Did she tell you she was leaving because of you? Is it possible that she left because she was looking for an excuse to not be there, and you gave her the excuse? What you did is establish boundaries of what was acceptable and what wasn't. You informed her that her attitude was unacceptable. Then you left it up to her. If she got upset, that's for her to deal with, not you.'

"That's one example of setting boundaries."

Session #3:

Vision Statement

I'm a healthy, vigorous man who divides his time between physical, mental and spiritual pursuits, and never runs low on energy. I make a great living from my creative writing career, which enables me to maintain a winter home in Key West, where I recharge my batteries and work on personal writing projects. I'm in complete control of my emotions, thoughts and actions and, therefore, my destiny. I consciously connect with the divine to serve others and myself, and though I love life, I'm not overly attached to the material plane. I always look forward to the next morning, but also take time to savor every moment of every day.

Dr. Lieber was pleased with my vision statement, mostly because I'd correctly interpreted his instructions. I didn't write a thousand-word essay in the subjunctive tense ("If I *were* rich, I *would* …") or qualify my statements with words like "maybe" and "might." Instead, I wrote "I *am*" this and "I *am*" that in five sentences. Perfect.

We spent the rest of the session talking about the wonderful events of the past week, which I've since forgotten. Guess they weren't *that* wonderful. Before we called it a day, Dr. Lieber also gave me some pointers on how to construct my Vision Pictorial, which was the next assignment.

"The vision pictorial is a short story about you," said Dr. Lieber. "I want you to expand your vision statement into a short story about your Best Self–

"No problem," I interrupted.

"—and tell me what you see. Do you see yourself on the shore near your beach house? Exhaust every possible verb that you can imagine. Exhaust yourself in the process. I want to know what the house looks like. I want to know if the breeze is blowing. What do you smell? What do you hear?

What do you taste? How do you feel? Who's with you? Make it as detailed as you can.

"So far, we've accomplished two things. One: we've seen where we are today, right? We've evaluated who we are and where we are – the likes and dislikes of our life. Two: we are moving to where we want to go. What is it that we want to achieve? What is it that we want? What does our Best Self really look like?

"When you read this short story to me, I want to be able to see you. Remember, this is all about you. This is your story. I'm here to coach you through it, but I can't coach if I don't know your game plan, and that's what this vision pictorial helps you create. I don't want you to give me excuses about how terrible your life's been and all the crappy things that have happened."

"Good," I said. "I did enough of that bullshit in therapy, and it didn't work. It was nice to vent, but in the long run, complaining didn't change anything."

"Yes, but that experience was good, because it eventually brought you to this point. The key is knowing that you cannot change yesterday, but that you have the power to change tomorrow. If you keep forward thinking – thinking how to create your Best Self and working to get there – you're making progress."

Session #4:

Vision Pictorial

Laura is lounging by the swimming pool, reading a cooking magazine, as I step onto the porch of our cottage in the Florida Keys. I've finished the first draft of the latest screenplay I've been commissioned to write, so I'm feeling content. I see the sun sinking over the palm trees on our lawn, which means it's time for my evening kayak tour.

Though I'm in great physical shape, I'm always keen to get an upper body workout by paddling through the clear, shallow waters near our winter home. So, I grab a pair of boating shoes and head for the dock.

"See you in an hour, babe," I call out.

> "Don't go too far," Laura answers. "I'm getting hungry."
>
> A fresh breeze wafts through my hair – streaked blond from months of salt and sun – as I paddle out of the canal toward open waters. Once outside the canal, I stop and let the kayak drift, savoring the aroma of citrus and brine, and the sound of waves lapping against the boat.
>
> As I gaze at the turquoise waters, the verdant plant life and multi-colored fish just beneath the surface, I reflect on my life's journey to date. After nearly 50 years of struggle, I finally allowed myself to be carried downstream by the Tao. The result was a spiritual, emotional and material metamorphosis that was nothing short of miraculous – achieving all the good things I've ever dreamed of in a near instant.
>
> I wonder whether there is such a thing as reincarnation, and if so, whether it will take me another 50 years in a future lifetime to find this kind of serenity. "Well, that drama that has yet to be enacted," I think. "Let's just enjoy what is, rather than worry about what may be."

Pretty cornball, eh?

Well, my assignment *was* to paint a verbal portrait of what I wanted. And this story represented what I wanted. I was also supposed to keep working on my vision board, but the only thing I'd put there was a photo of Ernest Hemingway's house in Key West. I *love* that house and I *love* Key West. This quirky little town has a big city atmosphere. It has a "screw the establishment" attitude that attracts assorted artists, writers, treasure hunters, oddballs, misfits and hard-drinking tourists. That was my kind of place. Of course, I wouldn't be spending time in the beer halls when I returned.

While writing the vision pictorial, I hesitated a few times. I wondered if I was being unrealistic by mentioning a *commissioned* screenplay instead of a spec script. Maybe I should make the work a history book or a novel? I'd be more likely to get those published than have a screenplay commissioned.

No, I thought. *This* is what I want. I want the movie script. I'll write the books later. Besides, this is just a snapshot of a *future* moment. It doesn't cover everything I'll accomplish over the next 40 years. So don't pull any punches,

Bruce. Don't treat the assignment as an exercise in wishful thinking. It's designed to help me create a blueprint for building my Best Self.

I buried my skepticism and finished the homework.

Dr. Lieber was happy with the assignment, and didn't have many comments. At first, I was annoyed by his lack of feedback, but then I thought, "What's he supposed to say? 'You're thinking too small! Don't you want to be a billionaire-astronaut with a supermodel trophy wife?' After all, this was *my* Best Self Vision, not his.

"We're going to look at motivators now," he said. "What is motivating you to want to do this? Deep down, why do you want to do this? Why do you want to change? Why do you want to achieve your Best Self? Are you doing it because somebody's telling you? Or are you doing it because you *want* to change and, if so, why?

"I've heard a lot of things from a lot of different clients. Some say, 'I want to be around for my grandchildren' or 'I'm just tired of feeling poorly' or 'I don't want to be sickly any more.' They are tired of this and tired of that. Those are great motivators.

"If you don't have a reason to change, if you don't have motivators to push you forward, then it's going to be like making a New Year's resolution. You're not going to be any different in a few weeks. Nothing will change.

"I want you to create a list of your main motivators in each of the four areas of your health – physical, mental, emotional and spiritual. Choose as many motivators as you want, as long as they are *the most important* motivators for changing that area of your life. If someone else wants you to change, and you agree it's important to change, list that as a motivator. For example, 'My wife wants me to change X, and because I love her, I think it's important to change X.' But don't list 'My wife wants me to change X, but I couldn't care less.' If you couldn't care less, that is *not* a main motivator."

I said, "Even if someone else wants me to make a particular change, I must really *want* to make that change, too, or it's not a main motivator. If pleasing someone else is my main motivator, it's okay to list that. But simply promising to make a change to get someone off my back is not a valid motivator. Is that it?"

"That's it."

In this session, I actually had *genuine* wonderful news. My lawyer had called to tell me that he'd struck a bargain with the state prosecutor. If I pled to second-degree assault and another misdemeanor charge, the prosecutor would recommend a suspended sentence and probation. To say this news lifted a *huge* weight from my mind would be an understatement. It lifted a *ginormous* weight from my mind!

The felony charges, which carried a combined maximum penalty of 100 years, had been hanging over my head for six months. I never thought I'd serve life in prison for a crime that caused no bodily harm, but I didn't want a jury to decide my fate. For one thing, I *had* assaulted my neighbor. I admitted this to the arresting officer and my lawyer. Fortunately, *neither* of them believed I'd committed *first-degree* assault or the other felony charges that the Commonwealth of Pennsylvania had piled on. In addition, my gun had been unloaded.

Anyway it seemed the nightmare was about to end. I just had to make a statement in front of a judge, and then let the complainants respond with a victim statement. My lawyer was convinced, however, that the neighbors wouldn't show up. Months earlier, he'd talked with them to gauge their anger level, and decided that they were more confused than angry about the incident.

Dr. Lieber congratulated me on dodging a bullet *and* drawing a valuable life lesson from the experience. I was a little irritated that he had so little to say about this momentous matter, but then I realized that we'd talked about it before, and he probably had clients who'd gotten into worse trouble.

* * *

I had to postpone my next session for three weeks, as I was suddenly "indisposed." Courtesy of the circuit court judge, I spent the next 18 days in the county detention center.

It could have been worse. Thirteen days were subtracted from my 30-day sentence for good behavior, double-bunking and participating in a work-release program. Also, the inmates and the conditions weren't as bad as the movies. I had lots of time for reading, including Wayne Dyer's *Change Your Thoughts – Change Your Life: Living the Wisdom of the Tao*, which Dr. Lieber recommended. On the minus side, the food was terrible and some of my "colleagues" were a little less than honest. In fact, some were borderline sociopaths who were getting ready to cross the border.

On the Monday after my last perception modification session, Laura and I drove to the courthouse, where we were greeted by an unwelcome surprise. The complaining neighbors had shown up. Minutes after the doors opened, my attorney entered with the prosecutor, smiling and chatting. When they noticed the complainants, they *also* seemed surprised. Soon, the judge entered and the proceedings began. The prosecutor read the charges, and recited a chronology of events immediately before and after my arrest. When she finished, the judge noted the plea agreement, and asked me dozens of questions about whether I agreed to waive this or that right, and whether I understood XYZ. I replied "Yes Sir" to each question. Then it was time for my statement.

I was sincere and honest. I thanked my lawyer for encouraging me to enter rehab and join AA. I thanked Laura for standing by me through years of alcoholism. I turned to face the complainants, apologizing for my outrageous behavior, and vowing to make amends per the Ninth Step of AA – "[Make] direct amends to such people wherever possible, except when to do so would injure them or others." I added that it was a shame we hadn't met under better circumstances. They remained stone-faced while I spoke, even when my voice cracked with emotion.

After I sat, the judge asked if the complainants wished to make a statement. The man did. He described himself as a quiet man who bore no grudges, especially since my gun had been unloaded. However, he believed that a lesson needed to be taught, and that probation wasn't enough. What if his girlfriend's children had been present! What would have happened then? They might have been emotionally scarred for life!

(*This* coming from a guy who used to scream obscenities at his ex-wife and children, and had served 18 months' probation for a DUI.)

My heart leapt into my throat. The judge was going to give me jail time. I *knew* that now. The only question was how much.

Thirty days, as it turned out. Despite my attorney's arguments, I wasn't allowed to participate in the work release program because I was self-employed. Note: After five days in a cell block, I was transferred to work release at the warden's discretion. Once you pass from the judge's territory to the warden's, the warden decides your fate. If he wants, he can release you from any sentence imposed by a judge. As a matter of policy, *this* warden tried to expedite the sentences of normally law-abiding citizens who'd screwed up without hurting anyone.

When the sentence was handed down, I experienced every emotion a human being can possibly feel – from rage and despair to relief and exhilaration. I was happy that the sentence wasn't severe. But I was furious that I would lose a high-paying freelance assignment. I was terrified of being housed with criminals. But I was excited, as a writer, to experience jail firsthand and talk with the inmates about their histories. I was torn between hate and empathy for my neighbor. Mostly, I was fearful about what awaited me in jail.

It was one hell of an experience, but I'll keep it short.

It wasn't as bad as *OZ*, but it was no day at the beach. Work release resembled a low-budget summer camp for incorrigible teenagers. What surprised me, however, was the keen intelligence displayed by many inmates. It was too bad, to repeat the cliché, that so many used their talents for evil and not good.

Within 24 hours of reaching the work release dormitory, I helped form a discussion group. It was composed of mostly middle-aged boozers and potheads serving short sentences. The exception was Tom, who looked like the Russian boxer from *Rocky V*. He was 22-year-old merchant mariner and – like the movie boxer – packed a wallop. With a single punch, he'd fractured the skull a college kid whom he'd seen abusing his girlfriend. In gratitude for his "heroics," a judge sentenced him to a year in jail.

Tom and I were the only members of the group who never left the dorm to pick up dead animals along the highway or sift through garbage at the local landfill. Because my stay in the dorm was less than two weeks, the corrections officer in charge asked me to clean the lavatory and mop floors whenever they needed it. That wasn't often. Tom was also given the job, along with several old men who were all nicknamed "Pops."

Anyway, we intellectuals gathered around our bunks each night to talk about every subject under the sun. We dedicated one night to pondering the Big Bang Theory based on this verse from the Tao Te Ching:

> Thirty spokes converge upon a single hub;
> It is on the hole in the center that the use of the cart hinges.
>
> Shape clay into a vessel;
> It is the space within that makes it useful.
> Carve fine doors and windows;
> But the room is useful in its emptiness.
>
> The usefulness of what *is* depends on what is not.[1]

At other times, we talked about why we'd ended up in jail, the lessons we'd learned, AA, NA, religion, politics, race, our adolescent sex lives, and

---

1   Dyer, Wayne W., *Change Your Thoughts – Change Your Life: Living the Wisdom of the Tao*. New York: Hay House, Inc., 2007, pg 57.

the care and feeding of marijuana plants. The last subject was usually raised by Stu – a big, affable guy who sounded like actor Seth Rogan.

Jack, the other member of our coterie, was fond of telling stories about his wild teenage days and his stint in the Marines, during which he contracted several STDs. Jack called me "Andy" (from Andy Dufresne in "*The Shawshank Redemption*"). Before long, *everyone* called me Andy, because I seemed like the white-collar type, and (in most of their opinions) had gotten a raw deal. I reinforced the stereotype by frequently imitating Thurston Howell III on *Gilligan's Island*. During mealtimes, I loudly complained that the "Chateaubriand is overcooked and the Cognac from an inferior year." I was also fond of saying, "Why can't someone make me an Old Fashioned the way dear old dad used to?" This never failed to get a laugh.

Thanks to the physical size of my friends – and especially because of Tom's reputation for pugilism (he really was a sweet kid) – nobody threatened me or said an unkind word. Of course, most of the younger inmates ignored the old farts. They were too busy getting in trouble. When they weren't being kicked back to "the other side" (the cell blocks) for sneaking cigarettes or tilting vending machines to steal 50-cent candy bars, they were stealing each others' stuff and getting into fistfights over some act of disrespect. My pals and I merely shook our heads at this childishness. Why would anyone risk getting sent back to the cell blocks over such trivial bullshit?

By the time my sentence was over, I was actually a little tearful at leaving my new friends. I was also filled with newfound respect and love for my fellow man. Few of the inmates I'd met made excuses for their crimes or blamed the victims. The vast majority admitted that they'd done something stupid and bad – whether it involved alcohol or substance addiction or attempts to make "fast" money.

Keep in mind that I wasn't locked up with the "hardened" criminals. The guys in my group seemed genuinely committed to turning their lives around. I hope our talks helped them do just that, but I don't know what happened to any of them.

Thinking of my neighbor, I realized that I held no grudges. I couldn't really blame him for having me arrested and seeing to it that I spent time in jail. He didn't know anything about me before the incident. He didn't know about any of the reasons that I snapped and behaved like a crazed maniac that July afternoon. *I* was still trying to understand why I acted like that! All he knew is that a wild man showed up in his backyard one afternoon, waving a pistol in his face. What was he *supposed* to do – invite me in for tea and scones? I'm lucky he didn't grab a gun and shoot *me*.

I was also lucky that my gun was unloaded, so I didn't accidentally end a man's life because I was drunk and angry over where life had brought me. Beyond the pain and anguish this would have brought to his family, I can only imagine how my punishment would have affected Laura and my family. I had a hard enough time figuring out how Tom managed to stay optimistic during his one-year jail sentence, much less what it would be like to serve a *life sentence*. Wow. There must really be a higher power watching over me. Someone sure saved my life, and it wasn't me.

On the morning of my release, Laura met me at the entrance to the jail. She kissed and hugged me. I nearly fainted. The sudden return to the outdoors zapped my brain. I needed a half-day to readjust to life outside the dimly lit jail. Every object was bright, shiny and a little strange. I was seeing the world through a new pair of eyes.

> Under heaven all can see beauty as beauty,
> Only because there is ugliness.
> All can know good as good only because there is evil.
>
> Being and non-being produce each other.
> The difficult is born in the easy.
> Long is defined by short, the high by the low.
> Before and after go along with each other.
>
> So the sage lives openly with apparent duality
> and paradoxical unity.
> The sage can act without effort
> and teach without words.
> Nurturing things without possessing them,
> He works, but not for rewards;
> He competes, but not for results.
>
> When the work is done, it is forgotten.
> That is why it lasts forever.[2]

This verse inspired me to continue building a better Best Self. It still does. But it wasn't easy – then or now.

---

2   Ibid, pg 8.

Session #5:

"It's been a while since I've gotten to speak with you," said Dr. Lieber. "I've been thinking 'I can't wait until Bruce gets back to his normal every day life.'"

"I wish I could say I was lonely, but I was surrounded by about 70 other guys, some of whom snored very loudly," I said.

"Well, at least you had the camaraderie."

"That's true," I laughed. "I met three very nice guys in the 'joint' – guys I probably would have befriended on the outside."

"That's good."

I was about to suggest that we review my main motivators, but first Dr. Lieber wanted to discuss another subject – that people tend to change *only* when they're faced with the threat of punishment or the promise of reward.

"Fear is typically the thing that counts for most," he said. "If our lives are going well, we don't ask how we got to this point. Fear is a mechanism that's built into everything that breathes. It's part of our psychological and physiological makeup. So when we ask, 'How did I get here?' we are usually looking at our lives from a fear-based perspective. For example, if a doctor tells you that your cholesterol level will eventually give you diabetes or a stroke, the fear prompted by that information may cause you to change your diet. Fear is your motivator to seek change."

"I know plenty about fear," I said. I was getting a bit impatient. I already knew about this stuff.

"A friend of mine used to drink too much," Dr. Lieber continued.

I thought, "I used to drink too much, too. Let's get back to business. I had three weeks to think about what we discussed in Sessions 1 through 4."

"He loved to drink and party until he was arrested for driving his motorcycle while drunk. He knew the risk of drinking and driving, but that didn't scare him. It wasn't enough to get him to stop. It wasn't until he was face-to-face with a judge – telling him he'd go to prison if he took another sip of alcohol – that he was finally scared enough to stop drinking."

"I can relate to that," I said.

"Good. Because people often need to relate to the vagrant on the street or the teen curled up over a heating grate before they become fearful enough to change. We need to empathize with such people, because *that* could be our fate if we choose to ignore the early lessons … the warning signs that our lives are spinning out of control."

"The motorcycle man scenario is exactly what happened to me," I said. "If I take another drink during my three years' probation, I'm back in jail. I was scared straight."

"And it all happened because it was *supposed* to happen at that time," said Dr. Lieber. "This is exactly where you were meant to be."

Despite my new outlook on life, I was getting annoyed with Dr. Lieber. Seriously, what did *he* know about getting tossed in jail? What did *he* know about getting in *serious* trouble, where the stakes are life and death, or freedom and imprisonment? As well-meaning as he was, the good doctor had probably never experienced more trouble than the occasional parking ticket. Was he capable of empathizing with what I'd been through – much less helping me work through the underlying problems that led me to this crisis? Was his perception modification and goal setting based on "field-tested" reality or was it just another pop psychology course stuffed with "feel good" platitudes and kindergarten goal-setting tactics?

I didn't say any of this. What I *did* say was, "Telling me I was meant to be where I am today sounds like a cop out. You didn't go through what I just did."

"Yes and no."

I said, "What do you mean, 'yes and no?' Have you ever been locked up for threatening someone with a gun?"

"As a matter of fact, yes. I *was* in prison for a couple of years."

I was dumbfounded. *Dr. Lieber? In prison?* But his voice was so soothing, and his demeanor was so calm. I'd never met him, of course. I didn't even know what he looked like. I pictured someone like Wayne Dyer – sparkling eyes, a smiling face, a non-threatening physique. I also imagined him as the 'friendly neighbor' – a Taoist version of Ned Flanders from *The Simpsons*.

"I don't share my bio with everyone," he continued. When I do, I usually give just a few 'lowlights.' But if you're interested, I'll tell you more about my history and how I came to develop the perception modification process."

"I am *definitely* interested," I said.

"Okay," he sighed. He paused, apparently mustering the strength to go on. "Before I begin, I want to stress that I *survived* these experiences. I'm not dead. I'm not living in a cardboard box, which is always a plus. Also, knowing that I lived through them gives me a sense of gratitude. I realize that I lived through these events for a reason. None of this was mere coincidence. I discovered the gifts hidden in these experiences – the life lessons that brought me to this point.

"I grew up in a dysfunctional family. My mother was 17 years old when I was born, and my father 18. He took off before my mother gave birth. At that point in her life, my mom was still a kid. She wanted to travel and do the things that kids do. She wanted to experience life. Unfortunately, she had a child, and that was me. So, I was moved around from place to place. I stayed with my grandparents; I stayed with my mother; I stayed with the parents of my mother's boyfriend. I stayed with friends or in hotels, and we traveled all over and did all sorts of different things.

"By the time I was 12 or 13, my mother had married. We were living in Reno, Nevada. My step-dad and mom were into drugs and drinking and the party scene. My step-dad was a biker and my mother was a bartender and Blackjack dealer.

"I can't say that my life was horrific, because it wasn't. I had a lot of great friends and family, but there was definitely dysfunction in the home. My mom and step-dad would get drunk or high, and for whatever reason, they wouldn't get along. There was a lot of verbal and physical violence. This went on for a number of years. Thinking back, I can't really recall a time when there wasn't verbal or physical violence.

"When my brother was born seven years later, I became the parent in the family, since my mom and step-dad were either working or partying at night. It was my responsibility – at least, I felt it was my responsibility – to make sure that my brother and I were fed, bathed, given clean clothes and so forth.

"I have a vivid memory from this period. Late one night, my brother and I awoke to the sounds of breaking glass and screaming. I told my brother, "Stay in bed" as I walked to the living room of our doublewide. There, I saw my mom and stepfather arguing. I also saw a .22 handgun. I yelled and lunged for the gun, knocking it onto the kitchen floor. I ran to the kitchen and picked up the handgun, taking it to the bedroom. As I was about to toss it out the window, my step-dad threw me to the floor. The gun flew from my hands. My step-dad was hovering over me, my mother behind us, screaming hysterically. We had a neighbor or a roommate, whose room was next to mine. On seeing the gun, he grabbed it and removed the clip.

"The next day, I went to school with bruises and a black eye. I told the school counselor what had happened, and child services placed me in a temporary group home. I stayed there for six hours before running back home. Then my mother called my biological father, and made arrangements for me to live with him in Colorado, which I did – for a while.

"By this time, I had learned how to survive, and it didn't matter whether survival required moral or immoral behavior. If I needed money, I could get it. Though I wanted a better life, and saw other kids living better lives, I didn't know how to change. Eventually, I got into trouble while living with my father, and went back to my mom, who was now living in Seattle. En route to my mom, however, I got into more trouble.

"After the bus stopped in Sacramento, there was a 12-hour layover until the next bus was scheduled to leave for Seattle. I was exhausted. I had no money or food. So I called my mom, who told me to find a soup kitchen. It just so happened that there *was* a soup kitchen nearby, so I got a bite. Afterward, I was hanging around the bus terminal when a gentleman started a conversation. I told him about my life – I told him I was broke and heading home after running away from my dad – giving him *way* too much information.

"He said, 'If you don't want to sit here, there's a county fair in town – the Sacramento Fair. We could catch a cab to the fair.' 'I don't have any money,' I said. He said 'Don't worry, I'll pay for everything.' I must have felt comfortable with him, because after we got in the cab, I asked if he had any alcohol. (I had already dabbled in alcohol and marijuana.) He said, 'I don't have any alcohol on me, but we can stop at a liquor store.' I said, 'Oh yeah, let's do that.'

"He bought a bottle. But when he came back to the cab, he said, 'You know, we can't go to the fair, because you can't be seen drinking. I have a room across the street from the bus station. We can go back there. You can have a few drinks and then walk back to the station.' I said, 'That would be great!'

"I clearly remember his apartment. You walked up a narrow and steep wooden stairway. Inside, there was a nightstand and a full-size bed. There were windows on every side of the room, and one side overlooked the bus station.

"He went in the bathroom for a couple of glasses, and poured some booze. I started drinking. It wasn't long before I was completely intoxicated – to the point where I nearly threw up. I didn't vomit, but I was very fuzzy-headed. At this point, the man started touching me. I remember feeling helpless and unable to fight back. So he molested me. When it was over, I collected my things, and returned to the bus station. When I arrived in Seattle, I didn't mention the incident to my mother.

"Soon, I was selling drugs and using drugs. At one point, I told my mom about what had happened in Sacramento. I don't know if it was a plea for help or what, but she didn't believe me. On that day, I left home and never went back.

"My life started to spin out of control. I was living from place to place – even on the streets. At one point, I slept in a parking garage between a mattress and the wall. I occasionally stayed with friends or in drug dealers' houses. Eventually, I met a man who let me stay in the vacant bedroom of his two-bedroom apartment north of Seattle. It became my crash pad for a while.

"Life was pretty chaotic. Some days were better than others, but I was slipping further and further into alcohol and drug abuse. And as you know, there aren't many happy endings when it comes to addiction. As the months passed, I stopped caring about what was right and what was wrong. I was willing to do whatever was needed to continue getting the drugs I was using.

"I was 15 years old. I'd dropped out of school. One of my friends worked at a fast food restaurant, and informed me one evening that the restaurant kept three days' worth of money in the safe. All I needed to do was show up. He and two other friends would pretend I was robbing them, and give me all the money. Well, that information turned out to be incorrect. I went to the restaurant, and hid behind a dumpster with a water gun. When a kid walked out with the garbage, I went inside to the safe, and my friends filled a bag with money. Then I got on my motorcycle and took off.

"The next day, I decided to get out of town. I bought a car, and took most of the money with me to Elko, Nevada. I went with another guy that I'd met. I had a friend who lived in Elko. She said we could stay with her for a little while. Before long, however, the local Sheriffs' department discovered who I was. There was a warrant for my arrest in Seattle for armed robbery. The kid who'd hatched the robbery plan had turned me in to the police.

"Soon, I was back in Seattle, in King County Jail, where I spent the next nine months awaiting trial as an adult – even though I was 16. While in jail, I remember sitting in a corner cell, looking out a tiny window at a Catholic church across the street. It's one of Seattle's most historic cathedrals. It was absolutely beautiful. I looked out that window and prayed: 'Lord, please get me out of this. I'll change my ways. I'll be a better person. I'll clean up. I won't do drugs anymore. I won't commit crimes anymore. I won't do any of that stuff. I'll go back to school. I'll go to church. I'll go to that church right there across the street.'

"The court convicted me of first-degree armed robbery, sentencing me to three and a half years in the state penitentiary. I was sent to Shelton, Washington, where I was put in protective custody because I was a minor. The first few months in prison were very scary. I had terrible nightmares.

I was afraid of every tomorrow. All I knew was that I didn't want to be there.

"After a year or so, I qualified for a work camp outside Olympia. It was a minimum security facility, so I was able to work outside and do interesting things in my spare time. While there, another inmate and I decided to escape from a worksite when the corrections officers weren't watching. We slipped into the trees and headed for the highway, where we were picked up by a trucker. That evening, we were in Portland, Oregon.

"I stayed in Portland for two or three months, working odd jobs, before deciding to return to Seattle. Once there, I hung out in the same area as before, but this time, I met a young lady who lived in Port Townsend, so I traveled there frequently. Eventually, I rented an apartment over there with one of her girlfriends. Shortly after we moved in together, we threw a house-warming party. Things got a little rowdy, and someone called the police. (I was using an alias, along with a fake driver's license.) The second time the police were called, I was arrested. And while I was in custody, somebody told them that I wasn't who I said I was.

"One of the officers came to my cell and said, 'We've gotten a phone call. The caller didn't identify herself, but she said you were not who you say you are.' For a while, I played innocent, but after he left, I had the opportunity to think. I knew the police just needed to run my fingerprints to learn who I was. Something suddenly overcame me. I was tired of running. I was tired of hiding. I was tired of the life I was living. I didn't know what to look forward to, but I knew I had to give up. I had to surrender my life.

"I pushed the button on the wall, and an officer came back to the cell. I told him who I was, and that I was an escaped convict from the work camp. Before too long, I was shipped back to Shelton. When I went to court over the escape, the judge had a couple of options. He could have sentenced me to three or five years for the escape. But instead, he looked at me and said, 'You know, I really believe you want to make a difference in your life.' This was after he had asked me if I wanted to make a statement, and I'd told him how I felt. So he said, 'I really believe you.'

"He sentenced me to one year, which ran concurrently with my previous sentence.

"When I went back, there were some struggles. At first, I still liked to play head games with people. But one day, after seeing the prison psychologist for a while, she said to me, 'I don't want to see you anymore. I'm tired of hearing you complain and whine about everything. When you're ready to take responsibility for your life and what you've done – when you're ready to make some changes in your life – give me a call.'

"*That* made a huge impact. To this day I remember looking into her eyes and seeing her sincerity. It was at that moment that I knew I had to make changes. I didn't know where I was going and how I would get there, but I knew there was something more – something I needed to do. For the remainder of my stay, I took college classes. I got my GED and took college courses available at the penitentiary. Eventually, I completed the barbering program. By the time I was released, I had my license, and I cut hair for a while. I also did a lot of soul searching.

"I spent three and a half years in prison. Before I was locked up, I was on the streets, into drugs and alcohol, and had no direction. When I was finally released, I was starting to mature and getting a vague sense of direction, but I was also scared – very scared of what the future held. I was told that, whatever I did, don't look back, never look back. On the day of my release, they took a group of us to downtown Olympia – to the Greyhound bus station. They gave me the money with which I'd come to prison. Then they gave me a bus ticket, and drove off.

"I went to Idaho, where I befriended some kids my age. I hung out at a swimming hole and ended up, you know, just being a kid for a while.

"Then, one of my friends and I decided to go to Alaska. We made it as far as Spokane, where I met my first wife. We were married for over six years, and had a son together. In the end, we drifted apart and got divorced. I was unstable at the time. I wasn't holding down a job and was flighty – still trying to live out my youth.

"I married again, but it lasted only a year.

"Soon after that divorce, my stepfather became terminally ill. I didn't have anything holding me to Spokane, so I packed the few things I owned in a duffel bag, and went back to Idaho. Once there, I stayed with my parents, and everything seemed to be going pretty well. I was reintroduced to a girl I'd met a number of years before. I became infatuated with her – to the point where I visited her every time I was in town. At times, she hid from me, because I was a little overbearing.

"One evening, we went out with some friends and, as I was making passes at her, she told me that she was unhappy. This made me angry, so I left. Early the next day, she yelled at me over the phone for being so childish. She'd warned me time and again that she wasn't interested in a relationship or getting remarried (she and her husband were separated). I replied, 'If we're going to talk about this, I'd prefer to talk about it face-to-face.'

"I went to her house, and we haven't been apart since. She got divorced, we got married a year later, and we had a beautiful child together. All told, we have four wonderful children. Before we were married, however, she said, 'If you're not going to settle down and grow up, I don't want to be with you.' That was one of the strongest motivators I'd ever been given, because I loved her with my whole heart. Because of that, I began to adopt her values. I settled down, and found a good job. My stepfather died, and shortly after that, my grandfather passed away, leaving me a small inheritance. My wife and I used the money for my education.

"I was acquainted with naturopathy and holistic medicine, and was interested in supplements and botanicals. But I think the biggest motivator to attend college was to fashion a solid identity. I had a great job, and was making good money. (I was a sales manager for a trucking firm.) But I had an identity crisis, and because of this, I was searching for a label. I wanted people to think that I was a good person. I wanted people to recognize me. I wanted people to respect me. So I thought, 'What better way to earn instant respect than to have a doctor's acronyms after my name and the word *Doctor* in front of my name?'

"The biggest shift in my consciousness came after a patient returned from a seminar in California. She gave me a pamphlet and a book. The pamphlet was written by Byron Katie, and was called *Loving What Is*. The book was Walt Whitman's *Song of Myself*. She'd been thinking about me, and thought I would benefit from the material.

"It wasn't until months later, when I was flying from Connecticut to New York, that I dug through my briefcase and came across *Loving What Is* again. As I read, I became overwhelmed. Something inside me changed, and it changed instantaneously. When I returned to Idaho, I called Byron Katie's offices, and had them send me DVDs and CDs and books and more pamphlets, so I could give them to my patients – and anyone else who wanted them.

"Everything just clicked. Everything came together. I knew I didn't have all of the information. I knew there was a lot more out there. But I no longer felt that I had to *be* something. Instead, I felt that it was okay simply to exist. I didn't need a label attached to me. I understood that my job was just a job. It's what I *do*, not who I *am*.

"My beliefs about myself were just beliefs. They weren't who I was. I didn't need to be a president or a CEO. I didn't need to be a doctor or a lawyer or any other occupation that came with a title. I just needed to surrender my life. I'd spent so much of my life trying to force life – trying to force myself in a particular direction. Now I knew what I was supposed to do and how to do it. Granted, my earlier work in medicine was designed to help people, and it was part of my journey. I was meant to do that. If I hadn't gotten involved in the field – if I was still working for the trucking company – I would never have met the patient who gave me the pamphlet. It was the one piece of information that focused me in a completely different direction. I realized that everything in life happens because it's meant to happen. It's all part of the journey.

"Today, I live one moment at a time; one day at a time. And I live my life in gratitude. Every morning, I wake up grateful for the opportunity to learn new things and touch people's lives. Every day, I do everything I can to listen to what life is teaching me. I try to pay forward as often as I can to friends and strangers.

"Surrendering yourself is *the most important* factor in all of this. I've been through AA and NA, and they're great, but I found that for every person there comes a moment when you're given an opportunity to surrender to life itself – to let the journey lead you in whatever direction it chooses. It's not always comfortable, because it often arises from adversity, but that's how we learn. We should welcome it, not fear it.

"I thought, 'Now I understand. Now I'm going to take responsibility for my life.' When you ask yourself why things happen, you become inquisitive. You search for reasons. That's what I did. And the more I searched for positive answers, the more those answers came to me. They came freely. I didn't have to search far. The next thing I knew, I was reading Byron Katie. And then I've got the Tao Te Ching in my hands, and then I'm reading Wayne Dyer's books and watching his movie. Suddenly, all of this information began flowing like a waterfall, and I stood underneath, receiving it.

"Sometimes, I would get frustrated with the wealth of information, because I couldn't find the connections. But once again, I had a revelation, and the connections between the materials presented themselves. Everything fell into place. How did the information from Byron Katie fit with Dr. Dyer? How did Dr. Dyer fit with Bernie Siegel? How did Siegel fit with the Tao Te Ching? How did the Tao fit into Jungian theories? Suddenly, all the information tied itself together and clicked.

"And when it clicked, clarity came to me. Life was simple. You're born, and you transition to death. Along the way is a journey. We learn our behavior and we learn from our experiences. And from those experiences, we graduate to the next level of our lives, and the knowledge we acquire from experiences is passed forward. We share the information we've acquired when we need to share it.

"We're born to learn and born to serve. We do these things because that's life. It's pretty simple: we love, we live and we die. We're not born to *be* something, because we already *are* something. Life isn't meant to be complicated and difficult. Life isn't meant to be confusing and frustrating. We're not meant to live our lives in fear. Unfortunately, we sometimes choose to write our storylines that way."

"So much for Dr. Lieber as Ned Flanders," I thought. I felt a kinship with him that I'd never had before. There was no question that he could empathize with my problems. There was no question that he'd crafted this program to help people like me. He'd *lived* the program. It had rescued him from a life that was once in the gutter – literally. This guy walked the walk!

We spent the last few minutes of the session reviewing my main motivators, but there wasn't much to say. I had nailed the homework.

Of course, I've always been good at acing tests and homework. It's too bad my mom and dad refused to give cash rewards for good grades – like many of my friends' parents did. I would have been the richest kid in school. But in our household, good grades were expected as a matter of course, as was college graduation and a career in management with a Fortune 500 company that offered cradle-to-grave security. As you can see, one of my physical motivators still speaks to my inbred desire for financial security – something I surrendered when I decided to pursue the dreams of an artist. But the desire for security is hardly unique. Nobody wants to live hand to mouth.

Main Motivators	
Physical:	Losing weight and achieving financial freedom (freedom from want).
Mental:	Refine ability to spot opportunities and avoid poor choices (in my business and personal lives).
Emotional:	Think before acting – i.e., become less impulsive.
Spiritual:	Allow the Tao to guide all of my thoughts and actions.

Session #6:

The next step was to review my main motivators again, and identify personal values and strengths that would help me build my Best Self, as well as obstacles and challenges that might impede my progress. Before we did this, however, Dr. Lieber stressed that it was important to reflect on *how* fear could support my main motivators.

"I've had you list what you want to change in all four areas of your health, along with reasons why you want to change those things," he said. "In addition, you've identified which of these reasons were fear-based, which reward-based, and which incorporated both. Today, I want you to consider fears and rewards when it comes to your main motivators.

"For example, you don't want to drink alcohol because of the potential outcomes. That would be one reason you want to change that behavior. It's fear-based. 'I don't want to drink alcohol because I'm fearful of the potential outcomes.' You may also find potential rewards in not drinking – you'll have a better relationship with your wife when you don't drink. So it's important to identify both types of reasons.

"Again, there are typically two reasons that people change their behavior. Fear, as we've discussed, is usually a better motivator because it's instinctive – it's built into all breathing creatures. Now we want to know how fear will work as a motivator, and transform it from a negative into a positive motivator for change.

"For instance, we've been able to identify that you want to lose weight. There may or may not be a fear motivator for that. You may have been told by your doctor that obesity increases your risk of heart disease, stroke, diabetes, or maybe you want to lose weight just to look better. If it's the former, you'll want to transform the negative into a positive motivator. 'I don't want to acquire heart disease or diabetes, so I'm going to achieve a healthy weight.' Use forward thinking to harness the fear and move toward positive outcomes. Sometimes rewards are forgotten or left out, so be sure to identify the *rewards* of losing weight. Losing weight can increase your productivity, because it will increase your energy, your clothes will fit better, you'll save money, etc. Rewards are good motivators – just not as powerful as fear-based motivators."

"I think fear can carry you only so far," I said.

"Usually, fear is an initial motivator, and then reward serves as a longer-term motivator," said Dr. Lieber. "Fear is short term; reward is long term. Fear gives you the poke that gets you going. It has the same urgency that propels the fight or flight response. For example, how do we help an alcoholic come to terms with his alcoholism? Well, life is actually the key motivator – typically through an experience or group of experiences. For instance, getting arrested and thrown in the clink can magnify fear to the point where an alcoholic makes the decision to finally quit."

"In literature, it's called an inciting incident," I said.

"Fear is an initiator of behavior modification," he said. "But after a while, the adrenaline wears off, and fear no longer has the same impact. What carries you through the change process is reward, which is why it's important to establish rewards."

"That's true," I said. "The alcoholics I've known have been more likely to stay sober once they transformed fears into benefits. Otherwise, they tend to become what AA calls 'dry drunks.' They abstain from alcohol, for a while, but since they don't see any rewards from abstinence, they usually relapse."

"In their minds, sobriety becomes a challenge," said Dr. Lieber. "All they see ahead of them is work and deprivation. Someone else is telling them they have to do this, but they aren't envisioning the benefits and rewards of the change."

"So abstaining from alcohol is seen as a deprivation, not a reward," I said. "I guess that attitude can apply to many behaviors."

"It applies to all behavior – *all behavior*," he replied "If you think about it, society has a tendency to formulate regional behavioral types, as well as racial, spiritual and other behavioral types. We acquire behavior because it's taught to us. And if you're taught a behavior, taught that it's appropriate, but later you're told it's inappropriate, you're not going to change unless you have an initial reason, and that reason usually revolves around fear.

"This is why the perception modification process is organized the way it is. As a matter of fact, I was just talking with another client before we started out session. He wants to quit smoking. His father smoked (but he eventually quit). Now my client wants to quit because he had a heart attack a few years ago, but the doctor says other factors actually caused the heart attack. Still, my client quit the moment the doctor told him that smoking *contributed*. The heart attack brought mortality to the forefront. That's the most compelling fear a person can have. Any time you shake hands with death, that usually does the trick. Unfortunately, he *did* relapse after a year."

"The urgency faded," I said. "Now the whole medical episode is nothing but a memory. Death is more of an abstraction."

"He didn't have the tools in place, so the fear dissipated, along with the likelihood of staying smoke free," said Dr. Lieber. "He and I talked about this today. The other aspect, of course, is that you quit smoking when you're ready to quit. Life will tell you if and when it's time. But do we want to wait until we have a heart attack before quitting? I'd rather spare myself the pain and the potential threat to my life.

"It's essential to complete this part of this program before moving forward. If I, you, or anyone can't identify the reasons behind our main motivators, the chances for success are significantly diminished. If you decide to quit smoking because your wife is on you about it, your friends are on you about it, your boss and your doctor are on you about it, but you can't say, 'I *want* to quit smoking,' your chances for success are minimal."

I said, "I know what you mean. I had to quit smoking in jail, since smoking wasn't allowed. But the first thing I did when I was released was have a cigarette."

"Right now is probably not the time for you to quit," he said. "If it were, you would. Okay. The next step is to identify any challenges you face in making your changes. This doesn't need to be in depth at this point. Don't overanalyze it. Just take a quick glimpse at the challenges. It could be that when you're stressed, you like to eat—

"—or when I'm bored."

"Right!" Take an initial look at how you can overcome the challenges. This helps you take an early look at how you think – where you are mentally. Remember, we're still in the discovery process, and during this phase, it's important to see how you think today. This exercise lets you recognize your 'here and now' attitude. 'This is how to of the how "I" think today. These are my current challenges, and this is how I can overcome those challenges.'

Session #7:

> ## Main Motivators
>
> Physical: Losing weight and achieving financial freedom (freedom from want).
> *Reasons Behind: (Fear-Based) Being overweight negatively affects my health, energy level and self-esteem. Financial want negatively affects my life and restricts my choices.*
> *(Reward-Based) Losing weight and gaining financial freedom will improve all of the above.*

Mental: Refine ability to spot opportunities and avoid poor choices.
Reasons Behind: (Fear-Based) I have missed chances to earn a higher income, improve the quality of my work, and enhance my social life because of linear, "status-quo" thinking.
(Reward-Based) I want to turn all of this around.

Emotional: Think before acting – i.e., become less impulsive.
Reasons Behind: (Fear Based) In the past, I've damaged my personal and professional lives through impulsive actions.
(Reward-Based) By exercising more thought and patience, I can prevent negative consequences and better direct my future.

Spiritual: Allow the Tao to guide all of my thoughts and actions.
Reasons Behind: (Fear Based) I no longer want to waste time "paddling upstream."
(Reward-Based) There's no better WAY to attain my dreams!

"Okay, let's take a look at the homework assignment," said Dr. Lieber. "There's not a lot to talk about, because quite honestly, you've made it very clear cut."

"Do you have to drag this information out of some people?" I asked.

"Sometimes, it's matter of getting people to focus. Often, I have to ask people to go back, take another look at the exercise and redo the assignment, because they just don't get it the first time around."

"It seemed pretty straightforward to me. What do some clients do wrong?"

"What they normally will focus on is … Well, here's a great example from a session this morning. I've been working with this woman for about four months, and she's stuck. The reason she's stuck is that she is constantly talking about her husband and her relationship with him. She always complains that he won't get more engaged in the relationship. What's happened is that she's become disengaged from her *self* and completely engaged in her husband's business."

"She was talking about what she wanted her *husband* to do?" I asked.

"Yes. She said her main motivator was, 'I want to work on my marriage,' but the main motivator *really* was, 'I want to change my husband, because I'm not satisfied with the way he behaves in our relationship.' I had to remind her that the process isn't about her husband or family. It's about her.

'We need to draw your attention to *you*. What are your motivators, your fears, and the rewards you envision? You can't change your husband. You can only change yourself. If that means your husband is walking parallel with you, that's wonderful. If it means he's not, that too is wonderful. We can't decide these things. Life decides these things for us. The only thing you can commit to is yourself.'

"This is a common obstacle, because a couple of things typically come into play in the middle phases of the process. One is that we've been taught to live in other people's business. We've been taught that we need to be engaged in other people's lives. We're living outside of ourselves. And by doing so, we neglect ourselves. But we're not able to change who we are, and reach the Best Self if we're obsessed with other people's business. It happens very often – with nine out of 10 clients. Many new clients put up a self-confident persona, placing the blame for their lives on others, but soon they have no choice but to focus on themselves. Eventually, it comes down to this: Are you here to work on yourself, or do you just want to whine? I won't let them whine. Go see a therapist if that's what you want.

"There have been quite a few times when I've sent clients away – referred them to counselors. I've told them that they're not ready for the program, not because of severe mental or emotional problems, but because they're too self-absorbed. They just want somebody to listen to them while they whine.

"I always remind people that this process is about *you*. There's going to be a learning curve, because it's become a habit to live outside ourselves. It isn't easy to take ownership of our lives. But if you aren't willing, you aren't going to gain the maximum benefits. You're going to rob yourself of the benefits you should be acquiring. When are you going to have time for yourself?

"Bruce, you've done a terrific job of identifying fear-based and reward-based reasons for wanting to change. This will take us forward to the next phase. Now that we've evaluated the motivators and the reasons behind them, look back and see if you want to modify your vision statement – that vision of your Best Self. Has the vision changed since you wrote it? Do you want to rewrite the vision statement and vision pictorial based on any changes we've made since that session? We're at a marker today. We can look back, and see how far you've already come.

"Do a little reevaluation. Your vision pictorial may be the same, or you may think, 'That was true back then, but now that we've completed this and that phase, things have changed a little.' One of the wonderful things about this program is that, since it's about us, we can go back and rewrite our Best Self. How's your vision board coming?"

"I only have the one picture on it so far – Hemingway's house."

"That's okay, but keep your eyes open. Keep building that vision of the house in Key West. What's on the grounds? Does it have a garden? Does it have a swimming pool? Find or create pictures of those elements. What about nearby beaches, restaurants and theaters? The vision board is a key component of creating your Best Self. Don't forget about it.

"As your next assignment, I want you to look at your personal values. Each individual has his own values, and when you start looking at where you want to go, you want to intertwine your values with your goals. Sometimes those values change, but it's something that must be recognized. In addition, you can pull some strengths from your values – things to support you in achieving your goals. As an example, the values you have been given or taught through the relationship with your Higher Power can help direct you toward your Best Self. It's important to identify any strengths that will help achieve your goals.

"We all have certain gifts and strengths. One could be the strength of endurance. Maybe we've been through a lot of adversity. 'Man, I've gone through a bunch of crap, but I'm still here.' So endurance is a strength we can use in this process. All we have to do is pull it forward.

"In the next exercise, I'd like you to explain in detail what your values and strengths are, and how these will help you achieve your Best Self."

"Can do," I said.

Session #8:

Values, Strengths & Gifts

My values, which I also consider my chief strengths and most cherished gifts, include:

- Honesty
- Integrity
- A keen sense of fairness and social justice
- Dedication to maintaining my values and pursuing my goals
- Empathy for others

- Perseverance when confronted with obstacles and challenges
- Hard work
- Loyalty to friends and family
- Life-long education and self-improvement
- A willingness to experiment
- (Suggested by Dr. L.) The gift of courageousness – to do things out of the ordinary

Here are some examples of how these values can support my goals:

Physical: *Losing weight and achieving financial freedom (freedom from want).*
Dedication and perseverance are (obviously) helpful in achieving these goals, but even more important is self-honesty. I have never – and will never --delude myself into believing that I've reached any goal before I have, and will never stop short and say "that's good enough."

Mental: *Refine ability to spot opportunities and avoid poor choices (in both business and personal life.*
My dedication to being a life-long learner and engaging in continuous self-improvement is what supports this goal.

Emotional: *Think before acting – i.e., become less impulsive.*
I've undergone enough trials and errors when it comes to the consequences of impulsive behavior, and seen enough rewards from forethought and careful planning, to achieve this goal. This goal is also supported by continuing self-education and self-improvement.

Spiritual: *Allow the Tao to guide all of my thoughts and actions.*
This goal is supported by my perseverance and dedication to life-long learning.

"Let's go over your values and strengths, and then set some short-term goals," said Dr. Lieber. "I won't go into a lengthy description of what short-term, medium-term and long-term goals are, because I know you're aware of what they are."

Dr. Lieber read aloud from my list of strengths and values. I stopped him when he reached 'willingness to experiment.'

"I don't know if that's a value," I said, "but I consider it strength."

"I consider it a value," he said. "A lot of people don't possess the gift of being able to step outside the box. You could actually take that one step further and call it the gift of courage or courageousness. It takes courageousness to do things that are out of the ordinary or that make you uncomfortable. You've done a good job of putting these strengths and values together. You've acquired some wonderful gifts thus far. Now the question is: How many of these gifts do you share with others?

"As you move forward, you'll discover how you can use these life lessons and gifts. We know that life is going to share these with us – that's how we learn and become adaptive and, in philosophical terms, that's how we become wise. But how do we use these gifts? How do we share them? *Do* we share them?

"We can do one of two things – we can either *live* in our lives or we can *exist* in our lives. At times, we have a tendency to get stuck, meaning that when we go through different experiences, we ingest them as negative experiences and then sweep them under the rug. We try to forget them. Therefore, we don't learn from them, because we haven't evaluated them for life lessons and gifts – gifts in the form of values like honesty and integrity.

"Strengths and values aren't just handed to you. You don't learn these in a book. You don't go to an honesty class. 'Today, I'm going to learn about honesty and acquire the power of honesty.' You acquire these through your social environment and experiences. If you come from a very honest family, you acquire this value from the experiences of being around honest people. On the other hand, you may be around dishonest people, and acquire honesty by *reacting* to their dishonesty. It depends on how you perceive the experiences. You could live in an honest family, but come to see honesty as unproductive.

"So now that we've acquired the gifts," said Dr. Lieber, "the question is, 'Am I going to be selfless or selfish?' The selfless individual is willing to share the gifts they've acquired because they understand that the gifts are meant to be shared. Selfish individuals choose not to share the gifts for whatever reason. It could be that an experience was too devastating and they can't get past it. They may not be able to recognize that lessons even exist. Or, they may recognize the gifts and aren't willing to share them, because they want to keep the memories to themselves.

"For instance, let's say a husband passes away and this was the best possible relationship the wife has ever had. And the wife is not ready or willing to let go of his memory. She's not willing to let go of the experience. Therefore, she can no longer engage in life. She can only exist. She's not sharing forward any of the gifts he gave her. She might have been in a lot of abusive relationships until they met, and then they spent a number of years together before he passed away. It may have been his entire purpose in life to reach a point where he shared his gifts with her – so she could know there were good men in the world, so she could feel loved and secure.

"Can you give an example of how you share forward a gift or value?" I asked.

"Sure. Let's say you're on the train heading into the city, and you sit down next to an individual, who is very sad. Because you've acquired the gift of compassion, you share forward that compassion by opening your mouth and saying, 'Hi, how are you? It looks as though you're not doing very well today. Would you like to talk about it?' Somebody who hadn't acquired the gift of compassion would never open his mouth. If you had acquired that gift, then you might learn that the person has gone through an event similar to one you've experienced, and you can share your empathy and comfort.

"Maybe they were heading into the city to find a bridge to jump off. I mean, we don't know how we touch people's lives. That person could be heading for a bridge to commit suicide, and your two paths were brought together so you would have the opportunity to share your compassion – to help them feel needed, loved and understood. Therefore, instead of heading for the bridge, she gets off the train and heads for a phone to call a family member or a friend. The only way that was going to happen at that very moment in her life was by life reaching out to her – through *you*. We do this on a regular basis without recognizing it."

"It sounds like the plot from *It's a Wonderful Life*," I said. "George Bailey didn't know how he'd touched the lives of others until he saw what would have happened if he'd never been born."

"That's absolutely correct. Once you get past your ego and the superego, realizing that all of the workday crap in your life doesn't have much meaning – you go to work because you have to, you buy an expensive car because it strokes your ego, but none of that will matter once you die – once you pop that ego balloon, you're left wondering: 'what the f— am I doing here?' Once you start wondering that, you have to analyze your life: 'I'm 30 years old, and I've had all these experiences. Why did I have these experiences? Why did I get into alcohol and drugs? Why did I marry this person?'

"At that moment, if we can be truthful with ourselves, then we can come to an understanding that the reason we go through these experiences is because that's how we learn. That's how we acquire the knowledge to move to the next stage. We have all of this knowledge, so what do we do with it? We decide to be selfless or selfish, that's what. You can hoard your money or share it. You can hoard it all you want, but when you're buried six feet under, it's going to become somebody else's money. It's not going to be buried with you. You're not going to spend it in the afterlife."

"Even if it was buried with you, it probably wouldn't stay there," I said.

"Exactly. The same thing applies to the knowledge you've acquired. Many times, we don't even acknowledge what gifts have been given to us. We don't even touch the surface of what we've been given, because we're so caught up in trying to reach a destination that can't be reached. Life is an endless road, but for some reason, many of us fool ourselves into believing that if we have another $10,000 we'll be happy. It's this foolish hedonic treadmill. While were on the treadmill, we forgot what life is really about. If you're one of the few who has just an ounce of insight, you can achieve true freedom. When you step off the treadmill, the question that's always been in the back of your mind – 'What am I doing here?' – is answered. It has nothing to do with selfishness. It has nothing to do with the superego. It has everything to do with the cycle of nature, with sharing forward. Somebody out there could benefit from the information you have. If you hoard the information, you are trapped in the darkness.

"In our cases – yours and mine – we've acquired compassion because somebody else has been compassionate to us in our dark hours. Somebody took time from their schedule to offer help. They didn't have to do that.

"One of the reasons I was drawn to working with you, Bruce, is because I can sense these gifts in you. We have a lot in common. This doesn't make us superior beings, though it probably makes us happier. It means that we've chosen to find meaning in the life experiences we've had, and to pass that meaning on to others. Part of that meaning may be teaching others to find the same meanings we've discovered.

"For me, this whole process started when that prison psychologist said she was sick of my whining."

"Is that what you tell some patients?" I asked. "'I'm sick of your whining?'"

"Not in those words," he said, "but I don't let people get away with whining. I have a patient that I've been working with for quite some time. Her husband passed away 11 years ago and she's been doing fabulously with the process. She absolutely adored her husband, especially since her previous relationships were very abusive.

DR. RICHARD A.M. POWELL

"But since he died, she's been stuck in mourning for 11 years. So she came to me, and has been doing very well. But when the 11th anniversary of his death arrived, she relapsed into all-consuming grief and self pity. She came in last week, and told me that she was stuck. I've heard the story over and over, so this time, I said, 'You're being selfish. You're telling me that you had five years with this wonderful man. He gifted you all of these wonderful things that showed you how to lead your life, but for 11 years you've ignored them to wallow in misery. Why? The only reason I can see is because you're selfish. You're existing in life, not living it. When are you going to get over it? When are you going to move on?'

"Sometimes, it takes a kick in the pants to force people out of a funk. For all this time, she's held herself hostage, held her emotions and memories hostage. It's like sitting in a dark room watching the same old film over and over again.

"Instead, why not evaluate the gifts he shared with you. If his entire life was dedicated to showing you how to have a better life, you're throwing that gift back in his face. How would that make him feel?

"She thanked me for opening her eyes and being honest.

"Most people are fearful of being honest. I don't have a problem with that. I'll be brutal. I can sit here and pussyfoot around and try to avoid hurting your feelings, but is that benefiting you or holding you back? Sometimes you have to be cautious and gentle. I've been working with this client for two years, so we have a relationship. I wouldn't say to a new client, 'Hey man, get over it.' But sometimes it takes brutal honesty. I was tired of watching her deteriorate because nobody in her family would be honest. I see her family members, as well. But they won't tell her how they feel and how they see her – she's closed herself off. They comfort her and give her words of encouragement. But is that helping or hindering? Sometimes it's a matter of coming forward, in a loving and caring way, and telling the brutal truth."

PHASE 3: OBSTACLES, CHALLENGES AND STRATEGIES

"Action may not always bring happiness, but there is no happiness without action."—Benjamin Disraeli

Session #9:

My homework assignment was to list my short-term goals in each of the four areas of health, and identify potential challenges/obstacles to achieving them. I was also supposed to list ways to reward myself when I achieved a daily goal, as well as "restrictions" that would apply if I failed to meet a goal.

I interpreted "restrictions" to mean a form of punishment, though Dr. Lieber didn't like the term punishment. *He* defined restriction as a task (or tasks) that I would find uncomfortable. For example, if I didn't meet my daily goal of avoiding too many snacks, I couldn't have dessert the following night *and* I'd have to perform 30 or 40 minutes of exercise. I don't consider exercise a punishment, but unless it's part of a hobby like golf or gardening, it's not on my daily agenda.

Unfortunately, Dr. Lieber had finally found an assignment that I wasn't able to breeze through. It was difficult for me to come up with appropriate rewards.

"Maybe this is based on some deeper psychological issues," I said, "but it was almost impossible for me to come up with rewards, except for the physical realm."

"Most people have a difficult time with this exercise because they don't know how to reward themselves," said Dr. Lieber. "How many people reward themselves on a regular basis?"

I said, "The only rewards I could think of were playing computer games, renting a DVD or having some kind of treat," I said. "And food is one of my problems, so that didn't seem like a good idea. Most of the rewards I considered were things I do anyway. I mean, when I have time, I'll always play a game of *Civilization* or watch a DVD. I guess I'm not good at denying myself things when they don't cost much."

"Let's begin with the physical aspect," said Dr. Lieber. "This is where a little self-control comes into play. You enjoy desserts, and who doesn't? I think you've actually got the hang of it, since you've created a nice reward. If you stick to your diet plan, you allow yourself a low-calorie treat at the end of the day – maybe after dinner. Where you're going to have a challenge is that you'll need to exercise self-control throughout the day, instead of walking to the refrigerator to have a bowl of ice cream whenever you want. Once you've established calorie counts and a dietary program you're going to follow, you need to stay within the parameters of the program. A dessert should become a reward for you. If you slip, then your no-dessert and more exercise restriction is terrific. You did a fabulous job in that area."

"I'm a little unusual in that I rarely eat breakfast," I said. "I'm not even that hungry until after dinner. It's then that I go crazy – stuffing one thing into my mouth after another until bedtime. One thing I originally put into the plan was forcing myself to wait 60 minutes before having a dessert, so the 'satiety reflex' could kick in."

"If that's something you want to implement, you certainly can do that," said Dr. Lieber. Here's another issue. Your physical short-term goal is to lose weight. That's a very broad goal. When we set goals, it's important to be specific. If I say 'I want to lose weight,' I've lost weight if I lose just one pound. Then I can negotiate with myself, and before I know it, I'm back to my old habits. That's why it's important to set specific goals. 'I want to lose five pounds in order to weigh 165 pounds.' Now you've set a specific goal instead of simply saying, 'I want to lose weight.'"

"I see."

"Obstacles. One common obstacle is using good behavior on a previous day to rationalize failure on the next. Stay focused on the goal – 'I want to weigh 165 pounds' – and the obstacles to reaching it. 'I really like dessert, so one of my obstacles is my sweet tooth.' Again, be specific in identifying your obstacles. 'I enjoy fast food.' That's another obstacle. You want to be very definitive in establishing obstacles.

"Now we move into the mental health arena. Here, your goals and obstacles are also too vague. We want to refine them. You've written, 'Refine the ability to spot opportunities and avoid poor choices' Hone that down. What is the real goal here? Come to a very concrete and specific goal. Currently, what are you really saying? You're saying, 'I need to keep my eyes open and be more intuitive.' But what does that have to do with a mental goal? Well, you could narrow that down to 'become more intuitive.' Now you've developed a more precise goal. Then, you could establish a more specific goal that would support intuition. 'How could I become more intuitive? Well, I could become more intuitive by becoming less assertive and more accepting. I will listen to others, I will listen to my surroundings, and I will be less apt to speak first.' So your mental goal could be 'to shut my mouth and listen.'

"If you're always speaking before you think, keeping your mouth shut will help you become more intuitive. It will give you the chance to absorb information from others and your surroundings.

"Remember, the mental realm is anything from the neck up, whereas the emotional realm moves from your groin to your neck – anything you *feel* in the form of butterflies or lumps in your throat, etc. *Thinking* before acting supports a *mental* goal.

"Now let's move into the emotional aspect, which is anything you *feel*. As an example, maybe I've determined that one of my challenges is judging, and that one of my challenges is anger or insecurity. It's a feeling. When you can put the word *feeling* in there, you know you're working on an emotion. So, if you w ww ant to feel more secure, happy and joyful, I'll start by identifying where I am today. Today, I feel fearful and I'm insecure. I read about things, and I'm full of stress.

"So I choose one problem, break it down and define it. Then I establish my goal. From there, I create a plan to reach the goal.

"Let's say I have feelings of insecurity, which stem from fear and a lack of self worth. So, my goal is to write a positive affirmation every day. That's it. It doesn't have to be long. It can be simple. I could say something like 'I am a good person.' That's it. *That* would be my goal, which would support everything I'm working toward. A reward for writing that affirmation is simply giving me a hug."

"Nice," I said.

"I'm coaching you to open up your mind. I want *you* to establish your goals and rewards. You must decide why you're setting the goals. 'Why am I writing this affirmation? Because I'm not happy with myself, so I need to constantly remind myself that I'm a good husband, a good father, a good friend, a good listener. I like myself. When I look in the mirror, I see a person who's been through a lot of obstacles and challenges, but I've made it.' Your affirmation will be a constant reminder.

"What are the obstacles that could get in the way of writing the affirmation? 'I have a busy schedule, and don't have the opportunity throughout the day. I drive to work, I'm busy at the office, and I don't even have time to eat lunch.' Once you've identified obstacles and challenges, go back and strategize through them. Assume that writing an affirmation takes two minutes. Do you have time? Of course! Put a pad of paper or a journal on your night table, and write the affirmation before you go to sleep.

"The more strategizing we do, the better the odds of achieving our goals.

"Then create a restriction. 'If I don't write my affirmation for the day, not only do I have to write one tomorrow, but I have to read it five times during the day to remind me how important it is to write my affirmation.

"In the spiritual realm, you have the same issue: the goal is too vague.

"Keep in mind that when we start short-term goal-setting, it's important not to take on something too big. Don't bury you teeth in a huge goal. Short-term goals are daily goals. They shouldn't take longer than 10 minutes to complete. If your short-term goal is too big, you're probably creating a mid-term or long-term goal.

"When it comes to losing weight (your physical goal), you may want to define losing a total of X pounds as your long-term goal. But what is your short-term goal?"

I said, "Well, I was thinking of going on vacation in April—"

"Great. Now, back up. You could easily lose a half-pound per day, right?"

"That would be about 500 fewer calories a day," I said. "That's doable."

"Now you've established a daily goal. To lose one or two pounds per week would require you to lose 300 to 500 calories per day, dropping your total calorie count to about 1,300 to 1,800 calories per day. That's a specific goal. And if you do that, what's your mid-term goal? How about losing two or three pounds a week? And for your long term goal, you could lose four to eight pounds a month until you achieve your target weight."

"I will definitely revise this exercise as soon as possible," I said.

"Great. Before we go, what wonderful things have happened since last week?"

"Well, I finished my outpatient program," I said. "It's almost too bad, because I really enjoyed the classes. They gave me a chance to meet new people and socialize – something I haven't done for years. But more important, I have absolutely no desire to drink anymore. Of course, drinking still intrudes on my dreams. I often have dreams where I'm desperately trying to buy enough booze for the weekend, going from one liquor store to another."

"Do you eat late at night?" asked Dr. Lieber.

"Yes."

"That may be causing vivid dreams. If you ingest food anytime within four hours of going to sleep, your body is still processing that food. When you sleep, your body functions slow down, but you're still pushing your body to process the food. If you ingest high-carbohydrate foods, you get a sugar spike while you're sleeping. *That* often causes vivid dreams. If you stop eating late and give your body at least four hours to process the food (and eat higher protein foods), the dreams should go away."

"Good to know," I said. "But I don't mind the dreams. They remind me of … what did you call it before … the 'here and now' way of thinking I once had. They're almost like a vision board of how I used to be. Keeping that vision board in front of me is a deterrent to drinking."

"Very good."

Below is my revised assignment, which Dr. Lieber and I discussed in a second installment of Session #9, which took place a week later.

Short-Term Goals
(And Obstacles to Achieving Them)

Physical: *Lose one-half pound per day until I reach 190 pounds.*

Goal: Consume 1500 – 1800 calories per day.

Reward: A low-cal dessert.

Restriction: No dessert the next day if I fail the previous day and/or I must engage in 30 - 45 minutes of exercise – such as vigorous walking.

Obstacles: These include: my love of fast food, a desire to get out of the home-office (buying lunch is a great excuse), my love of desserts and a tendency to eat one snack after another without pausing between them.

Mental:	*To be a more active listener – in both my business and personal life.* Goal: When talking with a client, friend or family member, WAIT for the person to pause before talking. Reward: Take a short break during the day to watch a favorite TV show or play a computer game. Restriction: Must watch 10 minutes of a Fox News opinion show (which will illustrate what it's like to talk with somebody who doesn't listen.). Obstacles: I have a tendency to get excited and interject ideas/opinions, sometimes try to boost my ego by demonstrating my command of the topic and/or "winning" the argument.
Emotional:	*Find healthy ways to overcome impatience.* Goal: Meditate or engage in breathing exercises before acting on impatience. Reward: Post a complaint in the elance chat rooms. Restriction: Immediately perform a chore I've been postponing – like cleaning the bathroom, the stove, etc. Obstacles: Feeling there's no time and/or that I must act to correct a situation immediately, forgetting to meditate or breathe.
Spiritual:	*Allow the Tao to guide my actions.* Goal: Perform a kindness for somebody every day. Reward: Ask the universe for a favor. Restriction: Read one verse of the Tao if I fail. Obstacles: Focusing too much on ME and my ego – e.g., any feelings of anger, frustration, exhaustion, envy, etc.

"Very good, Bruce. You've nailed it this time," said Dr Lieber.

"Thanks."

"I know that the rewards have been a struggle. Like most people, you aren't used to giving yourself rewards. Some people run out of rewards. One thing you can do is create a compound reward. Rather than having a reward assigned to each area, you can create a compound reward that encompasses all the goals. So if you meet all your daily goals, you are rewarded. If you don't make them, you don't get rewarded. This makes things a little less complicated, since it can be a challenge to find a good reward for each area of health.

"I didn't mention this in the last session, because I wanted you to get used to working with the rewards process – to open your mind and become a little more adventurous. If I told you from the beginning that you could use a compound reward, you would have just tried to think of one reward."

"I'm glad you did it this way," I said.

"It's also important to choose a reward you really like. Many people have problems because they're not used to rewarding themselves or they're *too* used to rewarding themselves. If they want an ice cream cone, they just get one from the freezer. The key is finding something that you like a lot, but that isn't a necessity. Choose a daily reward that you're used to getting, and turn it into something you must earn. Just don't turn your daily meals into the reward.

"I have a patient who looks forward to 30 minutes of Bible reading every day. She's been struggling to find appropriate rewards, so now the Bible reading is the reward. It's no longer something she expects.

"The restrictions don't have to be comparable to the reward. In her case, we'd find something she dislikes but that wouldn't be harmful – like doing the dishes. Normally, she and her husband may do the dishes on alternate days. From now on, she has to do an extra day of dishes if she doesn't meet her daily goal.

"One thing you can do, which I've found to be helpful, is to make up little cue cards. Every day, I flip through those cards to remind myself about my goals. This works like the vision board – the more often you see it, the more real it becomes.

"Now we're going to look more at obstacles and challenges from the perspective of past experiences and events. Fortunately, you've already done this. For example, you know from past experience that you love the taste of fast food and because buying it gets you out of the house. Otherwise, you feel stuck in your home office, which is a great excuse. You also identified a tendency to eat one snack after another without pausing between them. These are examples of how you've reviewed past experiences to identify obstacles and challenges to your goals.

"Now let's strategize through these challenges, and we do this by tackling one challenge at a time. When it comes to fast food, you need a strategy for overcoming this obstacle whenever it presents itself. So you're sitting at your desk, working on an article, but you're getting bored and need a break. So you think, 'A cheeseburger from Burger King sounds good about now.' What are we going to do next? The whole process of strategizing is to *not* wait until the event takes place, because then we are challenging our willpower. 'I know that I shouldn't have a cheeseburger, but it sounds so good. Oh, what the hell!'

"Unless you have strong willpower, you'll cave in, making excuses to convince yourself that it's okay to do this and that. So, rather than waiting until the urge develops, we're going to preplan. When you're sitting at your desk, bored out of your gourd, what will you do? One plan is to have a lunch pail next to you with your entire lunch – celery or carrot sticks – right there. You can grab them and go for a walk, which takes care of getting out of the house. Then, you could remove all the desserts from the house and put in replacements. Take out the unhealthy, and bring in the healthy alternatives. Always have a bag of veggies with you at all times. Remember though, if you eat them all too quickly, you'll exhaust your calories for the day. This will only happen once or twice until you learn to spread your food out evenly throughout the day.

"Strategize through each obstacle you've identified. Also, distinguish between challenges that are goal-oriented and challenges that are reinforced by past behaviors and experiences. Goals that are reinforced by past experiences are, for instance, emotional eating. People who have endured some kind of trauma in their lives often eat to comfort themselves. When they get stressed, they head for the refrigerator."

"Finally, your assignment for next week is to start assembling a support team. Contact between two and five people, and ask if they'd be willing to support you for the remainder of this process, which means indefinitely. You may already have such a support team in place naturally – your wife, friends and family – but I want you to formally organize your team on paper. Create a short list of the people in your support team (after you've contacted them and received their permission). I also want you to establish boundaries with each and every team member."

"Boundaries? I'm not quite sure what you mean by that," I said.

"When we establish our support team, it's very important to establish boundaries, meaning that these are your expectations, this is what you're asking, and this is what you're *not* asking. For example, 'I want to use you as a member of my support team. My expectation is that when I'm feeling vulnerable and need to call you, I can call for support. Is that okay? But if I *do* call, one boundary I'd like to set is that I just want to talk with you. I don't want you to give me your opinion on the situation.'

"I'm setting boundaries and guidelines with my support team, because I will need someone to talk to when I'm confused and frustrated."

I thought for a moment and said, "Could I also compartmentalize my support team, so that I only discuss certain subjects with certain people, and not others? For example: when it comes to business, I often ask Laura questions like, 'I think a client is asking for more work than I agreed to. What's your opinion?' *But* it's not a good idea to tell Laura that I'm having trouble making money, because my income impacts her personal life. If I complain that I'm not making money, she always panics and starts looking up jobs for me in the classifieds. Well, I'm not looking for a new job. I'm looking for emotional support."

"Absolutely. Feel free to set different boundaries with different people, each of whom have different levels of interest in your well-being. I ask clients to choose a support group of three to five people, so there's some variation in the mix. You may be comfortable having Laura as a support person in certain areas and not others. Another individual can serve as a support person in those areas. Yeah, you're right on task."

"So when I want to bitch about crappy fees, I can call my sister Kate for support, because she's also a freelancer, but not Laura, since she has a personal stake in my income. And forget my sister Joyce. I can talk with her about personal things, like my relationship with Laura, but since she's a doctor, she doesn't know a thing about living from paycheck to paycheck."

"You can't ask for pitching advice from a basketball player," said Dr. Lieber. It's also important to set boundaries because when you have a crisis, everyone's going to have his own opinions. Will those opinions help or hinder you? Usually, your head will spin. That's why I suggest you limit people's ability to offer opinions. You could say, 'These are my goals, and I'd like you to remind me about them whenever necessary. When I feel vulnerable to booze, I *don't* want you to tell me what a bad person I am, but to be loving and supportive.'

Session #10:

"I just realized that I never had you do a certain exercise – one I usually ask clients to do near the beginning of the process."

"Oh damn," I laughed. "And now we have to start all over?"

"Nothing that drastic. This is an exercise designed to help you understand and come to terms with your ego. Coming to terms with your ego is an ongoing process, but I usually assign the exercise at the start of the process.

"For one week, every time you say the word 'I' or 'me,' or whenever you refer to yourself by name or a personal pronoun, make a checkmark on a pad of paper or in a journal. Try to make it through an entire week without referring to yourself. When you refer to yourself in the first person, *that* is your ego stepping up and making itself known."

"Sounds difficult."

"This doesn't mean you're going to have the ability to immediately control your ego. Even when you're a seasoned individual, you won't always exercise complete control over the ego. But when you start to recognize the ego for what it is, you'll be able to say, 'I probably need to work on this a bit.' Try the exercise for a week, and see how you do.

"Did you have an opportunity to speak with each of your support team members to get their approval and go over boundaries?"

"No," I said. "I just made the list, because these are people I've relied on for years to provide the support and advice you're suggesting. This support team was created long ago, along with the boundaries.

My Support Team + Boundaries

Laura: My wife offers solid support in the areas of mental and physical wellness, since she's intelligent, educated and disciplined. In the past, she's offered valuable advice on handling situations that might otherwise have caused me to act impetuously. She's also an excellent diet, exercise and health "guru."

Boundaries: Any aspect of my life that directly affects her need for financial and emotional security is off limits.

Kate: This sister is a good source of emotional support, mostly because her life has followed a similar trajectory to mine (in terms of adversity and successes). She's also good at viewing the situations of others objectively. Probably comes from being a newspaper reporter.

Boundaries: Avoid talking about subjects that I wouldn't want repeated to other family members. I suspect that she can be a little "leaky."

Mom:	Great spiritual advisor, though she's a Christian and I'm not. She should have been one of the apostles writing letters to Corinthians or whomever.
	Boundaries: Avoid arguments about theological specifics, as well as emotional issues, since she tends to shut down when emotion enters the picture.
Joyce:	Youngest sister is also a steadying influence when it comes to mental wellness, as she's very analytical and can see the view from "30,000 feet."
	Boundaries: Like Kate, be careful not to reveal personal information that I wouldn't want the world to know.

"For example, my sister Joyce is a good source of support for mental wellness. She's very analytical, and sees everything from 30,000 feet. However, one of my boundaries is not revealing any information to her that I wouldn't want the world to know. She has a habit of sharing confidential information with others, and then claiming she was worried about me and wanted a second opinion. Good excuse, right?"

"Right," said Dr. Lieber. "It sounds like you've set the boundaries."

"I'm going to be seeing most of them next week at my mom's house."

"Good," said Dr. Lieber. "But even though you have long-standing relationships with these people, you should still ask their permission to become part of this process. When you ask permission, go over the boundaries with them. And I always suggest asking *them* if they have any boundaries. It's not a one-way street. They may not feel comfortable being a support person in certain situations and for certain problems. Don't step over *their* boundaries."

"You mean like calling them at midnight – like I used to when I was drunk?"

"Because of some people's experiences, which you may or may not know about, they may not be the best people to talk with about certain things. If you're aware of their past, it's likely you would sidestep the sensitive issues. But if they haven't shared certain experiences, you might step on their 'emotional toes' and get an unexpected reaction. For example, somebody who's been affected by child abuse may be hypersensitive to that topic. So ask if they have any boundaries of their own. Put all your cards on the table.

"In addition, it's important to define the benefits of having this particular team. What benefits can you find in talking with these individuals? You've already done that by, for example, saying that one individual is a writer, so she can speak to problems and challenges in that area. The *benefits* of having her as a support person include her understanding and experience of similar challenges and obstacles. It's easy for you to communicate, and you'll get reliable feedback. Write down those benefits to ensure your support team has been chosen for good, specific reasons – not just because you like them."

I said, "I've been aware for many years that it's important to have a support team. Do you often come across people who have few – or no – support people in their lives? You'd think, in your business, that one reason people come to you is because they have no support team to help them work through problems."

"Sometimes I find that individuals *feel* that they don't have a team. In those cases, we do the work together. This can be as simple as listing their friends. 'Well, I don't have any friends.' 'Okay, then let's talk about acquaintances – at work or church or school or in the community. Who do you associate with? Let's make a list of everyone you trust.' Then, we narrow down the list. Typically, a support team is anywhere from one to five people. I prefer three to five people, but that doesn't always happen. One person is better than none. I've yet to find anyone who couldn't find at least one person.

"However, I *do* tell patients to avoid listing children. Spouses and other family members are good, and friends are great. Sometimes you even need to find a counselor, a psychologist or a priest.

"I wish there were a better word than boundaries," said Dr. Lieber, "because I don't mean the term in a negative way. When we set boundaries, we're telling people what's acceptable and what's not. If a child spits in your face, that's unacceptable. If you don't set a boundary, he'll feel it's okay to continue that abusive behavior.

"We set boundaries on a regular basis, most of the time without knowing it. We don't appreciate stealing. If you have children, one of the virtues or boundaries that you set is 'stealing is unacceptable.' I guess we could exchange the word 'values' for boundaries, but boundaries is more specific. Boundaries allow us to facilitate open communication *without* being hurtful or having to lie to preserve people's feelings.

"Okay, now we've arrived at Phase 4 – exploring the past, searching our dreams and the unconscious mind."

"I've been waiting for this with baited breath," I said. "And I'm using live bait."

"Sounds messy. Anyway, this phase is the heart of the process, and it can get a little 'heavy,' because when we explore your dreams and your unconscious mind, we often unearth memories that we have been repressing. As we move forward in this process, I've found that a lot of clients begin having weird dreams. Very often, the dreams touch on repressed memories. The experiences, events and emotions are starting to work their way back into your consciousness.

"As your next exercise, I want you to write down any experiences that are still very vivid in your mind. In other words, the events might have transpired 20 or 30 years ago, but those memories come back very quickly. You can list as many as you want, but then narrow down the list to four or five experiences. By the time we've finished examining those four or five experiences, you'll have learned the techniques needed to work through any other past experiences by yourself. But for now, list four or five experiences, and summarize each one. I don't want you to go into great detail. Just explain what happened.

"As an example, one client can remember when she was three years old. She was standing at the back door, a screen door, and her father walked out. She reached up for her father, but he walked past her and picked up her sister instead. For some reason, that's always been in the forefront of her mind. It's something that has always bothered her. That's a good example of a memory. Certain events are always front and center in your memory. You can recall them, you can taste them, smell them, feel them, hear them. You can relive them very quickly."

"I know what you mean," I said.

"Once you've created your summaries, we're going to revisit those experiences. Remember, revisiting is not *reliving*. We are *not* reliving the experiences. There's no reason for you to go through that emotional trauma again. But we *do* want to revisit them. The reason we're revisiting those experiences and the reason I have you write them down is because *now* we're going to do some questioning. We're going to question the events. This is an investigative process during which we will depersonalize the events as much as possible, taking a very unbiased approach at questioning.

"Starting with the example I described, where my client's father walked past her to pick up a sibling, we launch a dispassionate examination by asking, 'What else was going on?' 'Well, at three years old, I don't remember. All I remember is reaching up and my dad walking past me.' So let's question the event. 'Is there a possibility that my sibling was hurt? Was my sibling crying? Was my sibling getting into something that could have been hazardous?' Question the event to determine if there were circumstances that we might have been unaware of when we experienced the event.

"The next part of our detective work is determining how the event influenced our lives. So here I was, raising up my hands toward my father. What kind of feelings overcame me? Maybe I felt abandoned or alone or forgotten, or whatever the case may be. How did that influence my life?

"Well, I became sympathetic for children left in foster care or other kids who were ignored by their parents. I feel attracted towards them, and want to be involved in their lives, giving them the attention they aren't given at home.

"Ask yourself, 'How did those events influence me?' Many times, we don't recognize how we were influenced by the events. Remember, we learn from experiences, so any experience will influence us from that point forward.

"Our next step is to identify the various gifts or life lessons that are hidden in those events. These events have bestowed gifts that we can now pull forward – gifts such as sympathy or empathy. 'Because I went through an abandonment event, I've always had an overwhelming desire to reach out to others who feel abandoned.' That's a gift of empathy, right? You feel empathetic and sympathetic to the needs of certain people.

"Now that we've identified the gift, now that we've gained insight into this experience, we go back to its roots. That's one reason that I have clients, who may have hundreds of vivid memories, chisel down their list to four or five – to the events that really stand out the most. What you'll find is that the experiences that stand out most are usually the 'root experiences' – the ones that shaped our perceptions of all other experiences to come. Those initial events were the most influential on who we became. After those events, the laws of attraction dictated that we would draw similar experiences into our lives.

"We go back to the roots, and we identify gifts. *You* are the one who will discover those gifts, not me. What are your gifts? What have you acquired? How do you use those gifts today? Are you an empathetic person? Do you have compassion? What do you *do* with that compassion?

"And then the key question. Are you ready for this?"

"Hit me."

"Do you believe wholeheartedly that you could have acquired your gifts without having gone through those experiences?"

"Probably not."

"Exactly. So most of us spend our lives looking back on these experiences in a negative way, but once we go through the discovery process, we can sit back and think, 'My gosh. I wouldn't be who I am today – a compassionate and loving person, who serves others – if I hadn't gone through this stuff. I might not have acquired the gifts.'

You couldn't be who you are today because these experiences made you who you are.

"Tell me your stories. Where have you been?

"Then we will *change your future* by modifying your perceptions of the past. As you can see in just the few exercises we've done, it's easy to start modifying how you perceive things once you dissect the reasons behind your perceptions."

"Right."

"One key to rediscovering your past is taking a big event and breaking it down into smaller segments. This is important because sometimes we will uncover other meaningful experiences – things so huge that they are almost bigger than us. But this discovery requires us to break down larger events into smaller segments.

"For example, one of my clients when she was a teenager worked in a church as the pastor's assistant for six years. And the pastor was –what would be a good word—"

"Behaving inappropriately?"

"Yes, behaving inappropriately. She continued to work with him because she was always trying to pacify her father. She thought so highly of her father but she also felt like he didn't recognize her achievements. So she allowed the abuse to continue because the pastor was giving her attention she didn't get from the father. She was getting male attention, even though it wasn't good attention.

"When we went through this particular phase of the program, one of the things she remembered was huge. We had to break it up into smaller story lines, and work through each of those until eventually we were able to see the whole picture.

"Sometimes the experiences you endure may not be for your benefit. That's an important concept to understand. Although every experience contains a personal lesson for you alone, sometimes we learn life lessons – and endure adversities and challenges – in order to pass them along to others. Three years after an event, you come across somebody going through the same thing, but they may not have the strength you had. So, it's through you and *your* experience that they can gain enough strength to overcome their own challenges and adversities. Sometimes, we are just a transporter – a carrier of information.   We're the messengers. We endure the experiences, we gain the knowledge from the experiences, we gather gifts, and what do we do with them? We can hoard them, but what fun would that be? So, we share them for the benefit of others.

"Why do we learn things? We learn them to pass them on. We pass them on to our children and our children's children. We pass them on to friends and loved ones. We pass them on to the people with whom we come in contact.

"They are teaching opportunities," I said.

"Absolutely. Here's an analogy I like to use. A woman's walking down the street in New York City, and a man runs up behind her, and snatches her purse. Her immediate response is to freeze. Then she screams. It's an involuntary response. A few moments go by while she evaluates what happened. Once the danger has passed, she now has a choice of lessons to learn. She can learn one of two lessons.

1. She can decide that, based on this horrifying experience, she's never going back to New York – or if she goes back, she's never walking down that street again. This lesson is based on fear and anger.

2. She might think, 'I wonder if that guy has been without? I wonder if he's got a family and they're living in an alley, and this is the only way he knows to make money to buy food. This wasn't about me. It was about him and his problems. I don't like what he did to me, but instead of reacting from fear and anger, I will recognize that this was a random event, and I'll learn to be more careful in the future.'

"The first lesson might prevent the woman from enjoying everything New York has to offer. In the second lesson, however, she recognizes that she needs to be more careful about personal safety, but she also realizes that the purse snatcher stole her bag for reasons that have nothing to do with her, that street or that city. The event that triggered both responses was the same, but the life lessons learned were completely different. One was negative and limiting; the other positive and instructive.

"This is why it's so important to reevaluate and question these seminal events to determine the bigger picture. One of my clients, as a little girl, overheard her father talking with a neighbor. He was complaining about the expense of having children. For years afterward, my client felt unwanted – felt she had been a burden on her family.

"When we reexamined the experience during the rediscovery process, I asked if she knew the context of the conversation with the neighbor. Was it possible that her father wasn't complaining about the price of child rearing – and about her – but was just upset that the price of food had risen, or the price of clothing or healthcare? Did the father withhold his affection on other occasions? Did he indicate at other times that he regretted having her. No? Then isn't it possible that she reacted negatively because she took his statements out of context?

"But because she interpreted his statements as she did, she worked extra hard to excel in school and in her career. 'You wanted to prove to your father that you were worthy. Would you like to undo your hard-won education and everything you've achieved since you were a little girl?' No. 'Isn't it interesting that your interpretation of this conversation changed your life in so many positive ways?'

"This is how we take a positive approach to the past. We reformulate negative experiences into positive ones. When we keep wrapping ourselves around a certain negative experience, we need to go back and reevaluate, reevaluate, reevaluate.   And one of the keys to reformulating negative experiences is by generating internal controversy. During this process, you may get a little upset with me. I may ask certain questions that you're not going to like. But it's by asking those questions that we make progress."

"Give me your best shots," I laughed.

"It's funny, because it makes you think, right? I may bring up certain things that make you think. I may piss you off, but you're going to *think*."

"I doubt that you'll piss me off. But we'll see."

"We will."

"I'm sure you could piss me off if you wanted to."

"You know what I'm saying. I may have to cause a little chaos – a little internal turmoil. I'm here to help you see things that you didn't see before. I'm here to help you see *why* you haven't gone from where you are today to where you want to be."

PHASE 4: REDISCOVERING YOUR PAST

"After a bitter quarrel, some resentment remains. What can one do about it? Being content with what you have is always best in the end."—Lao-tzu

Session #11:

After reflecting on dozens (maybe hundreds) of events that had occurred since I was two years old, I had gathered a lot of "raw material." Unfortunately, none of the memories seemed relevant to who I had become. At least, none of them were about experiences that I hadn't already dissected for their impact on my life. It seemed like I already knew myself backwards and forwards. I knew this couldn't be true, but I was stuck.

I gave Dr. Lieber a call.

After I explained my dilemma, he paused for a moment, and then said, "I wish more clients had your problem."

"Really?"

"This *is* one of the more difficult exercises, but when clients have problems, it's usually because they don't want to reflect on experiences that may have been uncomfortable – even traumatic. Typically, we wall ourselves off to a lot of memories, so it sometimes takes a while to open ourselves up to an honest evaluation of those experiences.

"But I've come across some instances of what you're encountering. A client who was molested by a trusted associate repeatedly told me that she didn't want to revisit that experience because 'there was nothing left to discuss.' In her opinion, she had already dealt with the fallout from those events, and the case was closed."

I said, "I'll bet she hadn't really dealt with it at all, had she?"

"Nope," he said. "And I'm sure you haven't recognized how many of your experiences impacted your life and worldview. You may *think* you know the impact, but I'm sure we'll uncover plenty of surprises."

"I'll have to take your word on that," I said.

"You have my word," he chuckled. "Just pick three to five memories that are very vivid – memories you recall in extreme detail – and which pop to mind often. The fact that particular experiences are always on the tip of your consciousness probably means that certain issues haven't been resolved. Trust your instincts on this exercise, Bruce. Don't over-analyze. You're a very self-aware person, but you have a tendency to over-think things."

"You're right about that," I said. "Okay, I think I can carry the ball from here."

"Great. I'll talk with you in a couple of days."

Per Dr. Lieber's instructions, I decided to summarize the first three to five memories that came to mind, as long as they were vivid and often intruded on my thoughts. All of these memories concerned events that took place between the ages of 7 and 12, but aside from that, they had nothing in common.

I didn't want to list memories that *seemed* important to my rational brain. I wanted to discuss memories that my subconscious continually brought to the surface, regardless of how insignificant they seemed. For this reason, I excluded one memory that may have shaped my attitude toward alcohol and partying...

I was six years old when my parents threw a party one Saturday night. I was sleeping in my upstairs bedroom when boisterous laughing and shouting woke me up. I trudged to the bottom of the staircase, where I saw that the dining room table was blanketed with liquor bottles, shakers, spoons and glasses. (This was the 1960s, when the middle class eschewed wine in favor of cocktails.) My father, red-faced and holding a martini-glass, greeted me with a rousing hello. He invited me to join the party, and began introducing me to his friends. But before he could finish, my mom ushered me back to bed. I remember being both frightened and intrigued by my dad's behavior and that of the guests. I'd never seen adults acting so strangely.

Regardless of whether that event contributed to my later bouts with booze, I didn't include it on my list. For one thing, I hadn't thought about that night for almost 40 years. For another, I'd already identified its impact on my life – that it introduced me to alcohol's mood-altering abilities when I was very young.

There were lots of other memories – joyful and traumatic – from which I'd also drawn lessons – lessons pieced together by revisiting the "crime scenes" much later, when I was more objective about the events. Over the last few years, Kate and I had traded childhood stories, helping each other recall things that we'd forgotten or repressed. But none of these retrieved memories were included on my list.

After a week of writing and deleting, writing and rewriting, I culled my list to three memories. Aside from the reasons given above, I wasn't sure why I chose them.

Memorable Experiences/ Events

1. When I was 13, a girl named Meg passed me a note, which said that her friend Natasha wanted me to ask her on a date. According to the note, Natasha would wait for me outside the classroom after the bell rang, so I could make my move. (NOTE: heretofore, Meg had devoted lots of time to making fun of me and calling me names, so I assumed this was a practical joke designed to make me look foolish.) After class, Natasha was indeed waiting for me, but I walked past her without a word. I heard her mutter, "faggot!" before she stormed off. Much later, it occurred to me that maybe this wasn't a set-up, and I'd blown a chance for my first date. I think about this all the time.

2. One boring afternoon when I was 10, I noticed my sister Kate walking down the hall, and decided to hide behind a wall and stick out my arm as she passed. This was something I'd seen in the movies. When I pulled this maneuver, she doubled over in pain, and began crying. I suddenly realized that this was no cartoon shtick. I'd really hurt her. Suddenly, my father came running to ask what happened. Kate told him, but before she could say that I didn't intend to hurt her, he said, "Let's see how you like it." He punched me in the stomach, knocking the wind out of me. Kate ran after him, crying that I hadn't intended to hurt her, but he never acknowledged the incident or apologized.

> 3. One powerful memory – I have no idea why – is of waking up one morning at my grandparents' house in Pennsylvania. I looked out the window on a summer morning, and saw an old-fashioned Ford pickup winding down the road past the house. I thought to myself, "What a lovely image. I could be in 1945 for all I know. Wouldn't it be cool if I were in a time warp?"

Despite my conversations with Dr. Lieber, I didn't really know what to expect from the next phase. I didn't expect to be hypnotized. (Was that even possible over the phone?) Neither was I expecting anything like past-life regression therapy, which is something I once tried with friends. We didn't visit a therapist. We used a book to guide each other into recalling events from our "past lives." It was a fun and fascinating experience, but it probably said more about our romantic notions of ourselves than it did about any past lives.

Anyway, I was a little nervous when I phoned Dr. Lieber that week. I wondered what his diagnosis of my memories would say about my past, present and future.

"There's nothing to be nervous about," said Dr. Lieber. "This is actually a training process. Once you learn how to work through your memories, you can use these same tools and techniques on your own."

"Oh."

"What we're going to do today is look at an experience or event, and learn how to get into an investigative mode to determine how the event impacted your life. Let's take a look at number one."

"That memory has been on my mind for the last 10 years," I said. "It comes up at least once a week."

"Since this experience has been on your mind for a long time, it's our job to figure out why," said Dr. Lieber. "Why does it keep coming up? Is there something we could identify that might free you from a revolving door?

"You've written, 'When I was 13 a girl named Meg passed me a note which said that her friend Natasha wanted me to ask her on a date. According to the note Natasha would wait for me outside the classroom after the bell rang, so I could make my move. Heretofore, Meg had devoted considerable time to making fun of me and calling me names, so I assumed this was a practical joke designed to make me look stupid. After class,

Natasha was indeed waiting for me, but I walked past her without a word. I heard her mutter *faggot* before she stormed off. Twenty years later, it suddenly occurred to me that maybe this wasn't a setup – that I'd blown a chance for my first date.'"

"I'd forgotten about this incident, but it popped back into my mind when I was in my early thirties," I said. "I suddenly thought, 'Wait a minute! Maybe Meg was serious, and that's why Natasha became so angry.'"

"Okay."

"Otherwise, why would she be so upset over a practical joke?"

"Right."

"For 20 years, it never occurred to me that this was anything but a setup," I said. "Then, one day, I realized that I might have made a huge mistake."

"Oh absolutely," said Dr. Lieber. "So now we want to *dissect* this event.

"Imagine you're an investigator – an FBI agent. This should be easy for you, since you've worked for newspapers and magazines. Let's begin by looking at the three characters in this experience: Meg, Natasha and you."

"Gotcha."

"What grade were you in?"

"Seventh grade."

"That would mean you were ..."

"I was in junior high school."

"So you were in junior high school, probably in the middle of the change."

I said, "If by *change*, you mean puberty."

"The hormones were flying, and like most males 11 to 14, you were probably very sensitive – to the point of hypersensitivity."

"No kidding? I didn't know that."

"Do you recall whether you'd become a little hypersensitive?" he asked.

"Yeah, but I'd always assumed it was because I had a tough time after moving from Chicago to Connecticut. I was basically a geek. I was often bullied during my first few years there. So, it's hard to tell if I was hypersensitive or just reacting to my treatment."

"And one of the individuals picking on you was Meg," said Dr. Lieber.

"Yes."

"She was one of the players causing that hypersensitivity."

"Yes – an antagonist."

"One thing I want you to know is that most boys between the ages of 11 and 14 are hypersensitive, thanks to the elevation and fluctuation in hormones. When you reach 15 or 16, things start to stabilize, and you're not as sensitive. There are other aspects, as you've mentioned, that also play into the hypersensitivity – that your peers made fun of you, for example. I just want you to understand and that you probably would have perceived this event differently if there had been no raging hormones."

"Probably."

"So Meg was one of the characters in this experience," said Dr. Lieber. "She was an individual who caused you grief in junior high school. Was she a popular person?"

"She had her clique, but probably not."

"Did you know her on a personal level or did you just know her at school?"

"I only knew her as a classmate."

"Did you spend the seventh and eighth and ninth grades with her, or was it just this one grade?"

"Those three grades in particular. Yes."

"Did she seem to pick on you most often through those years?"

"Yes. By ninth grade, we got along, though we weren't friends."

"But in seventh and eighth grades, *you* were the target? asked Dr. Lieber. "Yes."

"Had you ever been to her house or met her parents?"

"No, no."

"Did she have any brothers or sisters?"

"Don't know."

"Is there a possibility that Meg had older siblings?"

"I don't see why not, but I don't know."

"Do you have older siblings?" he asked.

"No, I'm the oldest," I replied.

"You're familiar, of course, with sibling rivalries and—"

I interrupted, "Oh yes – very much so. "Kate and I were academic rivals."

"So is there a possibility that Meg was jealous of you, and because she was jealous, she even liked you in a way?"

"Hmm. It's possible, now that I think back."

"And if she liked you, but was shy, maybe the easiest way for her to get your attention was to pick on you. That was her way of trying to draw your attention to her."

"Damn! She *was* cute, too. So I screwed up my chances with *two* girls?"

"It's possible that she liked you?" he asked.

"Yes, it is."

"And there's also a possibility that she had older siblings, or she experienced dysfunction in her family? Maybe she was belittled or abused?"

"Anything's possible."

"And because of the abuse she was seeing at home, because this behavior was being taught to her, and because she found you to be a 'weaker person,' she was doling out the kind of abuse she was getting at home."

"That's possible," I said.

"Those are possibilities," said Dr. Lieber. "The key here is that Meg's behavior may not have been about you."

"Today, I'm sure it had nothing to do with me."

"What's really interesting about this event, at least for me, is that here's this person who picked on you, but who was willing to set you up with Natasha."

"Possibly."

"If Meg really disliked you and was picking on you because she didn't like you, she probably wouldn't have gone through the process, or she would have tried to sabotage you rather than setting you up with Natasha. Maybe the reason that this memory has been continuous is because you were never able to figure out whether this event was a setup or an opportunity you overlooked."

"That is exactly right!" I said. "I didn't have a girlfriend until I was 16. But I suddenly realized, years later, that I'd had an opportunity when I was 13."

"The reason this memory has been troubling you is because after some time passed, you realized that you may have interpreted the situation incorrectly."

"To put it mildly," I said.

"Your initial perception was that Meg was trying to make you look stupid again. And the event has bothered you ever since, because the reality is that both Meg and Natasha may have liked you, but it took you 20 years to figure it out."

"I actually considered emailing Natasha a year ago to find out what happened, but I thought that might be inappropriate. Also, I couldn't get her email address. Can you imagine? 'Hi, Mrs. So-and-So. Remember me from 30 years ago? Were you really interested in a date?' She'd probably call the police."

"Chances are she wouldn't remember," said Dr. Lieber. "Or maybe she would."

"Now I feel bad. Maybe Natasha was being gutsy, and I shot her down."

"Could be."

"And after this humiliating rejection, she's pursued the wrong men ever since."

Dr. Lieber, "We can't know how this event affected her – if it affected her at all. But the next question is: why is this event always invading your consciousness? The obvious answer is that the 'was-she-serious-or-not' question still lingers, and will probably never be answered. That's part of it. The other part involves asking some questions about your relationships. 'Am I happy with my wife? Am I happy in my marriage? Am I happy with the friends, the family, and all of the intimate relationships I have?'

"If your relationships have been stagnant or there have been challenges, maybe the reason this keeps coming up is because you're wondering how you got into the relationships you have today. Maybe the image burnt into your memory is of a golden opportunity for happiness that you passed up. Life could have been better if you'd made a different choice at that moment."

"All of the above," I said. "It's obviously symbolic. I'm not going to ask Natasha to marry me."

"Right. Remember, we are exactly where we're supposed to be in our lives. You weren't supposed to be with Natasha. If you were meant to be with her, you *would* have had a relationship with her. If you were meant to be boyfriend and girlfriend – go on a date or share a first kiss – she would have continued to pursue you."

"That's true," I said. "She had opportunities. In high school, she was the best friend of one of my friends."

"So there were ample opportunities for you to get together, but you never did. Nothing happened because you weren't meant to be with Natasha."

"I know that now."

"Regardless of whether Meg was being sadistic or genuine, what difference does it make today? Does it really matter?"

"Not really," I said.

"You *did* choose correctly in that situation, because the choice brought you to this point in your life. The reason the memory keeps cropping up is because you *think* a different choice might have improved things, but it probably wouldn't have. In reality, this experience had very little impact. You didn't commit suicide. You didn't become a monk, right? It may have played a role in your teenage life, but moving into adulthood, how much did it really impact you? And that's the next step in this whole process – to ask, 'How did this impact my life? How has this impacted my life for the last 30 years?'"

"If anything, it created a positive impact," I said. "When I recalled this experience in my thirties, I became more receptive to 'disguised' opportunities. I also developed more empathy for what others might be feeling and thinking."

"Would you say that it helped you master the skill of intuitiveness?" asked Dr. Lieber.

"Yes."

"So when we look at the gifts you've acquired, one is intuition, which is a wonderful gift. You've also acquired the gift of empathy, as well as being open-minded and more accepting. You could even say that you've become more compassionate. That's four gifts right there. If we were to erase this experience from your life, is there a possibility that you might not have acquired those four gifts?"

"It's possible."

"Let's say that you were a popular kid in school. You didn't get picked on. Meg didn't even know who you were, and Natasha may have worshipped you from afar, but she never would have approached you. You came from a popular family, you drove a popular car, and all the popular kids liked you. Isn't there a chance that all of this popularity would have made you conceited?"

"A very good chance," I said. "My father once said that I was afraid of success, because I thought success would turn me into an asshole."

"I'm sure you've met people like that. Going further, consider how many decisions you may have made that were colored by this particular event."

"I have no idea."

"Is it possible that you've made multiple decisions in your life – in your relationships with clients, acquaintances and family members – based on this experience?"

"Yes."

"So now ... when we look at this experience, we can see that you've made some terrific decisions, thanks to an event you once viewed as a minor tragedy."

"I think the experience brought me to closer to others, and helped me refine my intuition. Because of the event, I realized that I was terrible at reading between the lines, so I worked on that skill. I never wanted to miss another opportunity like that again."

"Maybe it's time to re-evaluate your current relationships, and implement some of the gifts you acquired. Maybe a divine power worked through Natasha and Meg to give to you these particular gifts, so that you could share them forward."

"Maybe."

"What a wonderful thing," said Dr. Lieber. "Isn't it wonderful to know that you acquired these gifts instead of becoming an egotistical asshole?"

Between convulsive laughs, I said, "I guess."

"I'd go as far as saying that this has probably improved your writing skills. Intuition is one of a writer's key tools. It gives you the ability to see more than the average person. So now you see how we can revisit an experience without reliving it. We go back to the experience and look at it from different angles, asking the same kinds of questions we just did."

Session #12:

"Let's move to the second memory on your list," said Dr. Lieber.

"I'm looking forward to this one," I said. "Unlike the Meg and Natasha experience, I've only been able to draw a couple of lessons from this event."

"During this experience, you were just 10 years old."

"That's right," I said.

"And you were playing. You saw something in the movies and thought, 'I'm going to try this out and see if it really works.' You weren't being intentional. You wanted to see what would happen if you stuck your arm out and clothes-lined your sister. It's something you saw in cartoons and comedies."

"That's what I was thinking at the time."

"But once you nailed her, you suddenly realized that this was no cartoon. You'd actually hurt her. And along comes your dad, racing down the hallway, and he punches you in the stomach. And he never apologizes for this – even after your sister tells him that you didn't intend to hurt her. I'll bet he never acknowledged the incident afterward."

"No, he didn't," I said.

"Let's get into investigative mode," said Dr. Lieber. "What was your father doing prior to this event?"

"I don't know."

"Is there a possibility that he was having a bad day?"

"Oh sure."

"Is there a possibility that he was in a heated conversation with your mother?"

"Could be."

"Maybe he'd just gotten off the telephone with a colleague, or with the bank or someone else with whom he was frustrated."

"Maybe."

"Is there a possibility that when he heard your sister crying, and he came darting down, his blood pressure was up and his adrenaline pumping, because he thought something terrible had happened? You've mentioned that you and your sister were rivals, right?"

"Yes."

"So he races down the hallway, confronts your crying sister, and doesn't even ask what's happened. He just assumed, because of previous experiences, that you'd clobbered your sister on purpose."

"My sister began telling him what happened," I said, "but she was only able to say 'Bruce hit me' before he punched me."

"What did she say?" asked Dr. Lieber.

"She said, 'Bruce punched me in the stomach—'"

"And he retaliated before she could say anything more?"

"That's right."

"So he reacted without thinking," said Dr. Lieber. "He hears, 'Bruce hit me in the stomach' and he— Do you know if his mother was abused? Did he see his mom or other women being abused? Was he hypersensitive to men abusing women?"

"I don't think his mom was abused."

"Well, was your father raised with the belief that you never hit a girl?"

"Yes. That's something he taught me. And Kate sometimes used that to her advantage. She'd tease me mercilessly, knowing I wasn't supposed to hit her."

"Okay, so there are a few things going on here. It's possible that your father is already stressed out, hears your sister crying, learns that you hit her, and snaps. He punches you in the stomach and walks away."

"He had a habit of snapping."

"He had a bad temper?"

"Yes."

"Okay. So while the blow was directed at you, the reasons behind the punch may have had nothing to do with you."

"You know I never even *considered* whether or not he was having a bad day. There have been plenty of times when I've done things I later regretted – all because I was having a bad day."

"Other factors may have contributed to the violence."

"Sure. Like the fact that my parents had a bad marriage," I said.

Dr. Lieber continued. "He hits you in the stomach, and knocks the wind out of you. He doesn't acknowledge the incident. Well, maybe he acknowledged it, but he didn't apologize for one of two reasons. Either he was too stubborn to apologize or he felt bad about the situation, and just wanted to forget it."

"Probably the latter. I think he was embarrassed, but he was an Italian father. In those days, Italian fathers did *not* apologize for hitting their kids or admit to making mistakes in front of their kids."

"That sounds about right," said Dr. Lieber.

"It would have been hard for him," I said. "He never apologized for anything until I was in my thirties. One night, over some wine, he issued a blanket apology for my entire childhood, telling me he'd been a lousy father. Of course, he said that *his* dad wasn't much of a model either."

"So, he was a jerk during your childhood, and later he said 'I'm sorry for everything' at one time," said Dr. Lieber.

"It took a gallon of wine, but he did it."

"Good. Well, we know he was a volatile person. He had a bad temper. It could have been other stress factors. Did your dad show violent tendencies and verbally abusive tendencies at other times – when you weren't involved?"

"Not physically violent, but he seemed to have only two ways of reacting to negative situations – rage or silence. If you've seen *The Godfather* movies, the character played by Al Pacino was like my dad. He wasn't the type to display affection. He was like Vito Corleone: provide for the family, and let the women worry about the kids."

"Right."

"My dad was ruler of the house, and you obeyed his rules or else. The rules were whatever he said they were at any given moment."

"You didn't question if he changed the rules?"

"I sure *did* question them," I said. "That's why I was always in trouble. Kate paid lip service to 'the rules' to avoid conflict, but if I thought something was unfair, I'd make a stink – even knowing that I'd get 50 lashes with his belt."

"You were a rebel. And corporal punishment was common then. If a child misbehaved, you spanked him," said Dr. Lieber.

"Kate and I were talking about this recently, I said. "She said I was very emotional, and would never accept things the way they were. While she learned to 'go with the flow,' I rebelled from a young age."

"From today's vantage point, there's no need to personalize this experience, because hitting you was how your father dealt with you. He was raised to believe in corporal punishment, and he had a bad temper. Luckily, you were never hurt."

"That's true."

"Now we want to look forward and ask how this particular experience has defined you as an individual. How has it molded you as a person? Remember, behavior is learned, so it doesn't necessarily mean that you learned to be abusive. You may have learned quite the opposite."

"I think I developed a keen sense of social justice and a willingness to stand up for what I believe," I said. "I defended friends from bullies, and sometimes I got beaten to a pulp while my friends ran away. I wouldn't tolerate anybody trying to pick on weaker people."

"Very good. So as we look forward, we see how this particular experience, and similar experiences, molded your life. Instead of becoming abusive like your father, you became the opposite, because you didn't approve of his behavior.

"And now we're going to identify the gifts we have acquired. You already mentioned that you became a defender of the weak. Again, this is the gift of compassion.

In addition, you acquired a sense of justice – the desire to right wrongs. It's kind of like the lawman who stands up to the outlaws, regardless of the potential outcome."

"Like Gary Cooper in *High Noon*."

"You became an advocate for justice. That's a wonderful gift – a very rare gift. *Champion* would be a good word. Have you ever thought about this before?"

"No."

"It's a very, very rare gift. And these gifts are acquired through experiences. They're not given to you in school. You can't buy them online. The only way you can acquire these gifts is through the experiences you endure. And because of how you perceived specific events in your life, you became a champion for others. How many people have you known who'd be willing to take a beating for someone else?"

"One or two – maybe."

"Not many, huh? You stood up to bullies and took physical beatings while your friends ran off, because you were standing your ground for the weaker person."

"Yep."

"That doesn't happen often."

"I'm a total hero, man."

"We're all the heroes of our own lives – or at least the protagonists."

Session #13:

"Now we have a third and final memory to re-examine," said Dr. Lieber. "And it's a peculiar memory, because you're the only character in this experience. What's more, almost nothing takes place."

"Yes, but this is the oldest memory of the three, and it's also the one that pops into my brain most often."

"We're going to get into that investigative mindset, and review what we know," said Dr. Lieber. "First, you were seven years old. Second, you were staying at your grandparent's house. You wake up early one morning, and look out the bedroom window. You see an old Ford pickup winding down the road, and you watch it pass by. Is that it?"

"Yes."

"So those are some facts that we can pull out of this. And in this dream, you were thinking that you had entered some sort of time warp."

"It wasn't a dream. While I was watching this truck, I thought to myself that I might as well be living in another time. The truck was from the 1940s or '50s, and everything around me was very old. There was no physical evidence that the year was actually 1968 or '69. That's all."

"Okay. So you experienced an actual event."

"Yes."

"And your grandparents' house was in the country? It was a rural area at the time?"

"It still is rural."

"Okay, so those things are solid specifics that were present. You were looking out the window of your grandparents' house, you're seven years old, you just woke up, and after looking out the window, you turned away, and what you'd just seen was no longer there."

"Yes, the truck had passed by."

"How long did this event last?"

"A few seconds."

"Okay, just a few seconds. So you looked out the window, you just had awoken, and you saw this 1940's Ford pickup truck."

"Right."

"You weren't actually questioning reality."

"Oh, no. Not at all."

"So the question becomes, why is this memory consistently appearing?"

"Yes."

"What kind of relationship did you have with your grandparents?" asked Dr. Lieber. "Was it a good relationship or a poor relationship?"

"It was a very good relationship. I was there for nearly the entire summer. My family lived near Chicago, and this was one of the first times I'd ever been to Pennsylvania. I actually got carsick from driving up and down the mountains, because I was used to flat terrain."

"Was this a time in your life that was calm?"

"It was calm at my grandparents' house, but not at home."

"A very calming environment – maybe one that gave you a sense of enjoyment and well-being."

"Yes – a sense of enjoyment, well-being and security. My grandfather would take me fishing, I'd play baseball with my cousins, swim in the creek behind the house. Real Huck Finn stuff."

"Okay. And when it was time for you to leave and go back ..."

"I did *not* want to go back. During that time, my sister Kate and I were latchkey kids. Both of our parents worked, so we were left at neighbors' houses or with a string of babysitters. One of the babysitters was very nice, but the others brought their boyfriends over for make-out sessions. That upset us, so we'd hide in the basement or run off with our friends. Then, the babysitters would complain about what awful kids we were, and my parents would punish us. My mom sometimes weighed what we said against what the babysitters claimed, but my father always assumed that we were lying."

"So for those reasons, you didn't want to go back home when the summer ended. And that's because the relationships in your home environment were not ideal."

"No. And I just realized that this was the same year that my parents nearly divorced. They were planning to. That fall, my father took Kate and me to his parents' home in central Illinois, and those grandparents were going to raise us. I didn't know what was going on at the time. It was just an unexplained vacation. It wasn't until I was in my thirties that my father told me that his parents nearly adopted me."

I added, "When I was a kid, I thought I lived in a normal, middle-class family like the one in *Leave it to Beaver*. It wasn't until I was an adult that I learned how dysfunctional my family really was."

"As a kid, you were almost certainly aware that things weren't hunky dory, but you seem to have had a talent for internalizing these issues and then repressing the memories," said Dr. Lieber. "The behavior your parents considered incorrigible was probably you acting out in response to what was happening in the home. Your parents were oblivious to the reasons for your behavior because they were so wrapped up in their own problems."

I said, "Anyway, my parents reconciled. They didn't divorce until I was in college. But their marriage must have had an impact on the emotional tone around my house."

"Oh absolutely."

"I didn't pick up on the reasons behind these emotions."

"You were seven years old, and your parents didn't share everything with you. Okay. So here you are, at your grandparents' house. It was a very euphoric time for you. You had a great time, life was good, and you felt wanted, loved and secure. You didn't have the emotional confrontations that you had at home. There was no yelling, screaming and chaos. All of that was gone.

"One morning you woke up, you looked out the window, and here comes this truck down the winding country road. That memory is implanted in your brain because at that moment, you were experiencing euphoria. You looked out the window, and a feeling of calmness overcame you – that vision was associated with euphoria, with a feeling you really wanted in your life."

"That's absolutely right!" I said. "I'm amazed I didn't put that together."

"As life moved on, you *did* go back to your parents' house, you *did* go back to a chaotic environment with emotional distress, you *did* go back to school and back to reality. When you were with your grandparents, that reality disappeared. A different, idyllic reality took over. It was a perfect world. And then that perfect world went away when you returned home. And that perfect world has never materialized again. That perfect little world never came back. And when you went back to reality, you were left with that image and that feeling of euphoria you enjoyed for one moment. Today, it's just a memory."

Dr Lieber continued. "We always ask ourselves, 'Why do I remember stubbing my toe when I was five years old?' One of my clients *clearly* remembers an event that happened when she was three years old, even though she's in her sixties today. So we always ask ourselves during the rediscovery phase, why is that one memory so pronounced and what does that memory trigger? For that client, the memory triggers fear. For you, this memory triggers a sense of calm. A feeling of security and absolute calmness were burnt into your emotional memory."

"That sounds exactly right."

"The memory was recalled over and over, day after day, because you lived your life in chaos. And when life is chaotic, what do you refer back to?"

"A nice little anchor of security and calmness."

"You may want to put this in a journal," said Dr. Lieber. "Over the next few weeks, every time that memory pops up, take a moment to write down what's happening in your life."

"Is this something you recommend to many of your patients?"

"Oh absolutely. What you most likely are going to find is that every time this memory comes to mind, a certain type of event will be taking place. Just sit down and make a journal entry whenever this memory comes up. Are you stressed? Did you just have an argument with your wife? What's happening in your life? You don't have to be expansive – but briefly journal it. Do that for a couple of weeks.

"If you have this memory every day, it's going to be interesting to see the outcome – to identify the conditions under which this memory pops up. Once you've identified the conditions, you'll now know that this memory is used as a mental escape from XY and Z. And that will be your answer to the question: 'Why do I continue to have this particular memory?'"

"Gotcha."

"The reason you are having this particular memory is because that emotional memory is your escape from something. In other words, you're reflecting back on this moment because of something else. When you journal it, you'll figure out what that something else is from which you're trying to escape.

"Let's move to the next step. What gifts have I acquired from this memory? We've already identified one right off the bat. It's your personal escape. My guess is that you've probably used that escape to deal with a lot of adversity. When things got difficult, that memory provided a calming effect."

"It was my safe place," I said.

"And because that calmness allowed you to be more reflective, it's possible that you developed more patience because of this memory," said Dr. Lieber. "Because you were able to move into that image, it allowed you to be more patient with the situations you were facing instead of being explosive or violent. Given your history, there was nothing carved in stone that said you were destined to become a kind, calm and patient man."

I laughed, "I'm sometimes surprised that I didn't become a serial killer. I fit the profile at one time – an alienated loner with lots of anger issues."

"I can just imagine you as a child. There you are, with mom and dad in the kitchen. And they're fighting and yelling and arguing. You're getting scared, and you're angry, and this god-awful feeling is starting to wrench your gut. Then, suddenly, that emotional memory from grandma and grandpa's home comes to mind. You close your eyes, and what do you see? The tranquil image of an old-fashioned truck winding down the road in a country setting that Norman Rockwell might have painted."

"Or a Pepperidge Farm commercial."

"And you start remembering the moments you had – all those wonderful moments of fishing with grandpa, playing ball, having picnics in the backyard. It takes that wrenching feeling away. It makes you feel good. It gives you a sense of well-being."

"Yep."

"Now if you didn't have that memory, if you didn't have that escape, you would have sat there listening to all the arguing. That might have planted the seed of a traumatic memory instead of a pleasant memory to which you could escape."

"You know, that's very true. My sister Kate was emotionally scarred by my parents' dysfunctional marriage, whereas it never bothered me – at least not as much. I just escaped into another world. I wasn't always escaping into that memory, but I often played games that involved fantasizing. I once turned my closet into a submarine. I spent weeks in there, exploring the world's oceans and firing torpedoes at enemy subs."

"That was your coping mechanism. We all have those. And that's what that memory is from. It taught you how to cope with things. So that's another gift we've been able to identify. You acquired coping mechanisms through that particular experience in your life. Without that experience, you may or may not have acquired good coping mechanisms when the going got tough.

"So we've already identified two gifts," he said. "The next step, of course, is asking yourself how those gifts affected your life. How have they helped you from age seven until today?"

"Well, as you suggested, during periods of stress, I rarely respond with explosive anger or violence. However, I *do* tend to bottle things up, and once in a while – when the coping mechanisms fail – I'll explode. That's what happened when I got into the 'tiff' with my neighbor. The booze drowned out my coping mechanisms, and I went berserk."

"Right."

"Whereas I usually retreat into my own head."

"Right."

"I've been reading about a phenomenon in a marriage book by John Gottman. He says that men sometimes get 'emotionally flooded' when having arguments with their wives. In response, they engage in "stonewalling." They mentally shut down. My grandfather used to do that. I actually remember my dad's father being nagged by his wife. He just sat there, calmly reading the newspaper, without saying a word. He shut down, because he couldn't cope with the nagging. It's as if his mind said, 'I can't cope, so go ahead and scream. I'm not going to deal with this right now.'"

"Absolutely," said Dr. Lieber. "Now in the future, as you identify more experiences, the steps will always be the same. You always begin by going into investigative mode. In other words, you start asking all sorts of questions about the experience. It's important to be as thorough as you possibly can, as if you were investigating a crime. The more questions you can answer, the better. Try to gather as much information as possible, because that's going to help you reach a better understanding of the whole experience.

"The next step is to identify any gifts or lessons you've acquired. So in this last case, we learned through the investigative process that your home life really sucked. Identifying that fact was the *key* to unraveling the mystery of why the memory was recurring so often, as well as the gifts you acquired from it.

"Then we investigate how you have utilized these gifts, and what you've done with the life lessons learned. And we've also identified how the events impacted your life then and how they impact your life now that you've recognized the gifts and lessons that you acquired.

"Finally, you ask yourself if you could have acquired these gifts without having gone through that particular experience or experiences in your life."

"It seems like the answer is usually no."

"It usually is. That's one reason why we are always where we're supposed to be at any given moment in our lives."

Session #14:

The three sessions spent rediscovering my past introduced a level of clarity into my life that I'd rarely known. In addition to helping me reshape my perceptions of those events and recognize the gifts each event had bestowed, Dr. Lieber sparked another revelation: life is not all about *me*. That may seem like a '*duh!*' moment, but this realization helped me to finally make sense of many other memories.

I'd always interpreted childhood events from my *own* perspective, and with my own perceptions. I barely considered what the other people involved in the situations might have been thinking and feeling. I'd reflected on what *I* had done or not done, what *I* was feeling and thinking. As the protagonist in my tales, *I* was the one who bore the blame or the credit for the outcomes. It rarely occurred to me that *other* people might have behaved well or badly or strangely because of the circumstances *they* faced – circumstances often unknown to me.

I'd never thought about the stresses and strains my father might have been under when I was a boy. Aside from trying to provide for the family in the only way he knew how, he was only 21 when I was born. Not surprising, then, that he sometimes lost his temper and took it out on me. Since corporal punishment was a normal part of child-rearing then, it wasn't as though he was intentionally abusing me. It was perfectly acceptable and normal behavior during the *Mad Men* era. Not that I'm excusing his behavior. I was just able to put things into perspective after my sessions with Dr. Lieber.

For the longest time, I'd also believed that I'd ruined my chances with my first high-school girlfriend by making a clumsy pass on our second date. We'd gone to dinner that night, and come back to my house. There, we played video games and drank my father's wine. She leaned her head on my shoulder, but for some reason, I didn't interpret this gesture as a prelude to intimacy. Instead, another half-hour passed before she announced that she needed to go home. After I walked her to the car, I tried to kiss her, but she claimed she was tired. Within a week, she dumped me.

Using the investigative techniques I'd learned from Dr. Lieber, I revisited this memory, and came to a stunning realization. It was entirely possible that she broke up with me for reasons that had nothing to do with my clumsy kiss. In fact, it was possible that the break-up had *nothing* to do with *me*. Within four weeks of the break-up, a story in the local newspaper announced that her mother had "accidentally" died of carbon monoxide poisoning. Seems she "fell asleep" in her locked car in the garage. There were whispers throughout school that the death was no accident, but a suicide, as it was well known that her parents' marriage was in trouble.

For 30 years, I'd never considered the possibility that her home-life might have impacted her relationships with others. As obvious as this seems today, it just never occurred to me then. I was so wrapped up in what *I* must have done wrong that I never thought to ask, "Was anything happening in *her* life that might have caused the break-up?"

As I revisited one memory after another, I asked similar questions about other "characters" in my past dramas. Time after time, I realized that it was entirely possible (if not probable) that the other people involved in these events had contributed as much as me – if not more – to the eventual outcomes.

For all these years, I'd been trying to solve the mysteries of my past without considering *all* the facts. I'd been trying to analyze a game of chess by following the moves of just one player. I suppose we all do this at times, but I now laughed at my naiveté. As a creative writer, I should have known better than to analyze a storyline without examining the histories, motives and circumstances of *all* the characters. On the other hand, people usually need enough time and distance before they can analyze their own lives, so I decided not to be hard on myself. Besides, it was time to move forward with the perception modification process – not to dwell on past mistakes.

In our next session, Dr. Lieber and I reviewed the memories we'd discussed, and then talked about the value of rediscovery process in general.

"Rediscovering your past is the peak of the program," said Dr. Lieber. "Now you're prepared to move forward with all of the exercises designed to take you from where you are to where you want to go. What we're really after here is this: If you have memories that are potentially complicating your life – from childhood, early adulthood or even yesterday – that are inhibiting your progress in life, you must unlock those memories and evaluate them in order to move forward.

"Phase 4 looks at where you've been. You evaluate the experiences you've been through to determine what has shaped you, what is working for you, and what is holding you back. Not only does this bring you to a point of acceptance, but it also answers the questions, 'How do I fix this? How do I change this?' That's a key component. People were always telling me to fix my behavior – do this and do that – but nobody was there to give me direction, because nobody had a clue. Everyone just knew that my behavior was unacceptable to them.

"While reviewing some clinical psychology information, I came across a story about a guy who walks into a psychiatrist's office. He complains to the psychiatrist, "Everybody keeps telling me that it's all in my head." It was funny because the reality is: it *is* all in your head. But it's not in your head as a *mere* sensory recording of events – but as an emotional memory. An emotional memory has a physiological component within the limbic system. An emotional memory is a physical trigger. We acquire our memories from the five senses, and from that acquisition we develop emotional memories. And we use these emotional memories to protect ourselves in the future, but they can also hinder us. So the purpose of rediscovering our past is to alter our perceptions of experiences so we can reprogram emotional memories.

"For example, let's say your walking down the street when you're a teenager, and you're mugged by a guy with a goatee and long hair. Every time you see someone with a goatee and long hair, you'll get an unsettled feeling in your gut. So how do we change that? We do that by going back to that particular experience and asking the pertinent who, what when, where and how questions. We also take an unbiased approach, looking at the event from a position of distance as adults. The whole idea is to put a question mark in your mind. Normally, after an event has taken place, we solidify our perceptions, interpretations and conclusions of that event. We say, 'That was the way it was.' We must re-open our minds by removing the locks and chains that bind that memory in our minds. And we do that by asking all those pertinent questions. The whole process allows you to move forward.

"Do you feel the same way at this point, Bruce. Do you feel this was a pivotal point in the process?"

"Absolutely yes," I said.

"Because now we're getting into goal setting. And my thought is, 'How can you set goals and follow through if you're still mired in the muck.'"

I said, "It's like trying to paint a masterpiece on a canvas that is splattered with globs of old paint. You might succeed in creating a okay painting – considering what you had to work with – but it won't be the best painting you could possibly do."

"That's a good analogy. I strongly believe that this is the reason why most of us fall short of following through with goals and plans. We haven't dealt with a lot of this history. And because we haven't, and we have emotional memories that produce involuntary responses, we drive into these roadblocks again and again."

"I know exactly what you mean," I said. "For example, I've known for years that I have a problem with authority figures. Thanks to my perceptions of my father, I've never held a job where I didn't eventually have a run-in with the boss. But even though I've known this for decades, that knowledge never kept me from flipping my lid when the boss did something I considered tyrannical. Unless I had enough time to calm down, an automatic anti-authority response kicked in, and I'd be lucky *not* to get fired."

"That's a great example of what I'm talking about. And you saw a therapist at one time, didn't you?"

"Yes. I long ago identified some of the emotional memories that triggered unwanted behavior, but I never got any help in re-evaluating those memories and reshaping my perceptions so I could *overcome* them. Instead, I sat in the therapist's office, telling him the same kinds of stories over and over. I wonder ... are some people unable to even *identify* the events that hold them back?

"For example, when I criticize my wife – even constructive criticism – she completely shuts down. She shuts down, and stops talking, except to overreact. I'll say, 'I don't appreciate it when you call me a lazy scumbag, just because I won't get up at 5:00 a.m. on Sunday to vacuum.' In response, she shuts up. If I ask what's wrong, she blurts out, 'I don't want to criticize you, because obviously everything I say is wrong.'

"I've come to believe that something must have happened in her life that caused her to develop a thin skin. But I have no idea what it is. She was in therapy for almost two years, and her therapist couldn't identify the source of this, so ..."

"It could be a suppressed event that she doesn't know exists. Your verbal communication may be triggering an emotional memory, but not a *mental* memory of what caused those emotions."

"I can see where some people would hit a brick wall with your process."

"Well, if they do, then they're not ready for this program. From the very beginning, I ask clients, 'What do you want from this process and what are you willing to do?' A key component that I preach is that this program is for *you*, not for your wife, your friends or your neighbors. It is an empowering, self-centered program. Because you want to take control of life, and no longer have it control you, you have to be very honest with yourself. If I'm a client, and I'm not willing to be honest with myself, I should walk out the door.

"You can lie to yourself. You can try to manipulate the program, but the bottom line is that it's only affecting your outcome – nobody else's. So you have to go back and say, 'What are my objectives? Why am I doing this program? Why am I learning to use these tools?' If you're objective is to get your girlfriend back, that's probably not going to go over real well. If you're tired of living your life the way you have, the only way you can start to achieve that goal is to be honest with yourself. You have to be able to step back and take the position that, 'I know this is how I react to this experience, but I have to get into that investigative mode and look at this event as objectively as possible. I know that the excuses are no longer working, so it's time to be honest.' You must make a cold, calculating analysis based on exhaustive questioning – billions of questions. Ask every possible question covering every angle of the event or experience.

"I'm wondering how you deal with clients suffering from extreme guilt – people who desperately want to undo their actions or who keep reliving the same memories? For example, when I was a kid, I had a puppy that was always digging up the lawn. In response, I spanked her – sometimes until she yelped in pain. After a couple of weeks of regular spanking, I stopped because of something my grandpa said. But ever since then, I've felt incredibly guilty. I keep picturing my little puppy (who went on to lead a long and happy life) cowering beneath my raised hand – and I want to go back and stop myself from spanking her. For years, I've felt terrible about this."

"Well, what I would tell you as a client is that 'what's done is done.' For one thing, you were using corporal punishment on your dog because you were obviously taught that this is how adults 'corrected' misbehavior. And when your grandfather said something to you about it, you stopped. Is that right?"

"Yes."

"You didn't inflict any lasting injury on your dog, or maybe no injuries at all?"

"There were no physical injuries, but for the rest of her life, she cowered if I inadvertently raised my hand in that way."

"That's exactly what an emotional memory does. It triggers a physical reaction. A raised hand triggered the emotional memory of the spanking, which triggered a physical reaction. Bruce, what happened, happened. Beating yourself up isn't going to undo it. Use positive forward thinking. Consider the gifts this event brought into your life. It's obvious that it helped you acquire the gifts of compassion and empathy, or that these gifts were at least reinforced."

"True."

"When it comes to guilt, I recommend – if possible – following the AA model. One of the 12 steps is make a list of all of the people you've injured and make amends. Once an action has taken place, it's taken place. The damage is done. But you *do* have the ability to go back to those individuals, acknowledge that what you did was wrong, admit your remorse, and offer to make amends – be they physical, emotional or mental amends. Of course, if someone died because of something you did, you can't bring that person back to life. The only thing you can offer is emotional support to the family or loved ones. You can't undo what you've done."

"I suppose you could make it one of your goals to make amends."

"Oh absolutely. But here's the catch. Yes, it's something you need to work through in this program. If you have skeletons in your closet, you need to take them out. But you also need to forget about the person you wronged, and concentrate on fixing yourself. Always remember, this process is about forward thinking. If you feel guilty or believe you need to make amends, pick up the phone, make the amends, and move forward. Getting mired in guilt is a dead end. Treat the guilt as an obstacle or challenge, and work through it as you would any other obstacle or challenge. And once you're done, trash-can it. Don't reflect forever about this action and how you feel about it.

"This is a step-by-step process for working through anything in your life. To do that, you must empty the vessel so you have room for new experiences. If your bucket is full of muck, you won't be able to receive anything. There's no room. During Phase 4, you eliminate the emotional torment, guilt, anger and sadness. You work with the direct physiological component that is emotional memory. Once you develop the ability to reprogram your emotional memories, the rest of it is a no-brainer. I mean, I teach you how to establish and follow through with goals, but you can take college classes that will do the same thing. That's why Phase 4 is the critical component of this program – the phase that makes everything else possible.

"So now we're at the point where we can start making some changes. And we're going to divide it into the four areas of health – mental, emotional, spiritual and physical. Don't overwhelm yourself by setting a ton of goals. Make a list of all the things you want to acquire, and then prioritize them. You only want to establish one or two goals for each area of health. If you set 50 goals, you're chances of following through are minimal. You'll probably get so overwhelmed that you'll become stressed and annoyed, and you'll eventually give up.

"So your physical goal might be to eat healthier (more fruits and vegetables), and lose a certain amount of weight within 90 days. Micro-define your goals. Don't leave things up to interpretation or rule bending.

I always recommend that you don't set your goal any further out than six months. Ninety days is perfect. You establish your long-term goals. Boom. Simple.

"Then, you start working backwards from long-term goals to your medium-term and short-term goals. The long-term objectives help you establish the shorter-term objectives. We did this when we developed your weight-loss goals – losing one or two pounds per week to lose five pounds per month to lose 15 pounds in three months, etc. Now, you have all of your goals set.

"Then you just follow the formula – listing your motivators, strengths, values, setting up a reward and restriction for each goal, and so forth. Always be sure to establish that reward. This is something you've worked hard for. You deserve a reward. Make your rewards larger for the longer-term goals. They don't always have to be treats. Expand your thought process and get creative. Also, be sure to identify any potential obstacles and challenges, and develop strategies for overcoming those obstacles and challenges. That way, when you confront obstacles, you'll already have a plan in place to deal with them."

PHASE 5:
PLANNING AND GOAL-SETTING

"The reason most people never reach their goals is that they don't define them, or ever seriously consider them as believable or achievable. Winners can tell you where they are going, what they plan to do along the way, and who will be sharing the adventure with them."—Denis Watley

Session #15:

More than any other exercise, I struggled with this one. Setting well-defined goals for the medium term and long term didn't come naturally.

After reviewing my rough draft, Dr. Lieber said, "Remember that when we establish a goal, we're making a commitment. You did very well in the physical area. You said, 'Lose twenty pounds in three months.' That's your long-term goal, and you made it a statement. However, for your long-term mental goal, you've written, 'Think of ways to earn $3,500 per month' And for your emotional goal, you wrote, 'Find healthy ways to overcome boredom.' For the spiritual, you have, 'Allow the Tao to guide my actions.'

"So your long-term *physical* and *spiritual* goals are right on the money. But your mental and emotional goals ... you seem a little insecure with those, or maybe you feel a little weaker with them. Revisit those goals, and make them statements.

"I'm not going to 'think' of ways to make $3,500 per month; I am going *to make* $3,500 per month. We don't want to think about it. We want to do it. If we want to use this as a mental goal, then establish that you're going to earn about $40,000 annually by generating enough projects to average $3,500 per month. Make a commitment.

111

"Also, instead of choosing $40,000 annually as your long-term goal, set your long-term goal at three months. Reduce that $40,000 to $10,500. Now, even though it's a long-term goal, it's still a short enough duration to keep you on track. Working toward a 90-day goal keeps your mind engaged. Sometimes, we have a tendency to allow laziness to creep in when we set our timeframes too far out.

"When you look at 12 months, you might convince yourself, 'I've got 12 months. If it doesn't happen in the next few months, no big deal.' The next thing you know, a year has passed, and you're trying to figure out why you didn't achieve your goal. Ninety days brings more urgency to the task. When people don't reach their goals, it's often because their timetables were too generous.

"I'd like you to expand your mind even more. You've written 'think of ways' to earn this amount of money. Then you made a statement in your medium-term goal, which was originally set to $3,500 per month. How are you going to do that? How many contracts are needed to earn $3,500 per month? This will put everything into perspective. If you need four contracts for X number of dollars, then that's your medium-term goal. Maybe you need to be paid for writing a certain number of words or working a certain number of hours. So then you'll need to carve out a certain number of hours for research and writing versus new client acquisition. If you don't have any work, you're going to devote (say) four hours per day to getting new contracts.

"Now we have a road map from Point A to Point B. We now know what we have to do. We have a detailed plan of attack.

"As you meet each goal – daily, weekly and monthly – you've listed as your reward that you will get to save five dollars a day for a special vacation account. Stop. You will not 'get to save' the money, you *will put* that money into the account. FYI, this is part of that training process that 95% of us have to learn. That's because most of us don't make statements. We make insinuations. People tend to say, 'If I do what I'm supposed to, I get to save $5.' Well, that's an assumption, and we don't want assumptions. We want specifics. When I do x, I will *then* do y.

"What's missing here is a long-term reward. You have five dollars going into a special account, but I don't see the rest of it. So the mid-term reward would be putting $25 into the vacation account. But what's the long-term reward? How about taking the vacation? It could be a week in the Florida Keys. If you put $25 a week into the account, that's $107.50 multiplied by three. After a year, you'll have saved $1,300 for your vacation."

I said, "I can see why so many people never achieve their goals. I wasn't very specific about what I wanted or how to achieve it."

"Exactly. People tend to be too broad in setting their goals. They don't break things down. That's why so few people fulfill their New Year's resolutions. Nobody thinks about specifics. How many pounds will you lose each week, each month, each year, and what kinds of food will you eat?

"Weight Watchers is a terrific program because it uses these same principles. It has you set the goals, and makes you weigh in every week, which holds you accountable. It gives you guidance, tools and coaching.

"I hear this often in my clinic. 'Well, I was super busy today, and I forgot my lunch, and I couldn't get out of the office to get it, so I went to McDonald's and grabbed a big-ass sandwich and a gargantuan soda. Then, when I walked out of the office, the boss told me I needed to go to a dinner meeting, so I ordered a 16-ounce T-Bone steak with mashed potatoes and a dozen cocktails …'

"I sit there thinking, 'And your point is?'

"The bottom line is you have to be responsible for yourself. I'm here to coach you, but not to baby-sit. Step up to the plate and commit. Is your motivator strong enough? If so, then take responsibility. Stuff the excuses in your back pocket. Turn the process of working toward goals into a habit. Take control of life instead of letting life control you.

I said, "I think our society, over the past 30 years or so, encourages people to play the role of observers or victims."

"Absolutely," said Dr. Lieber. "And the irony is that people will learn to accept this kind of behavior as the standard. I really believe that we are spawning an uneducated, dumbed-down society. If we don't change it now, we're going to end up with a population like the one in the movie *Idiocracy*. When I saw that movie, I thought, 'Oh my gosh, we're almost there.'

"We need to teach people a few simple techniques using the simple tools of paper and pencil. They need to wrap their minds around the process of 'I can do this. This is my goal. This is what I want to achieve, and this is how I'm going to do it!' We already do this in our work environments. We don't just sit down and say, 'I think I'll write a 100-page report today,' and then hope that it materializes. We use goal-setting and planning processes. Why not incorporate that kind of planning into our personal lives?

"I'll be honest with you, Bruce. I used to be terrible. I used to be a fly-by-the-seat-of-your-pants kind of guy. It took a lot for me to train myself to do this process. But now I do it with everything. I sit down with paper and pencil, and list out everything I want to do. I break it all down, just as we did a few minutes ago. For example, I'm taking flying lessons right now. You certainly don't learn to fly a plane by sitting down in the cockpit and saying 'Fly!'

"I guess we also need to distinguish between goals we really want to accomplish and those that would simply be *nice*," I said.

"That's also the reason, in the front end of the process, that we start by asking 'where am I and where do I want to go?' Of course, that's going to change. You're going to modify yourself as you work through this program. But if you don't have an idea of where you want to go, or where you've been or where you are, how do you expect to put together any goals? My goal is to bring clients to this point, because the next phase of the program is putting everything into action. It's the Commitment Phase or Initiating Your Plan.

"We'll talk about that next week. In the meantime, rework your objectives."

Session #16:

Thanks to Dr. Lieber's advice, I was able to revise my goals without much fuss.

Long-Term Goals

Physical: Long-Term Goal: *Lose 20 pounds in three months.*

Medium-Term Goal: Lose approximately 1.5 pounds per week.

Short-Term Goal: Consume 300 fewer calories per day.

Shorter-Term Reward: A healthy low-calorie dessert.

Long-Term Reward: Buy a new suit that wouldn't have fit before.

Correction: No dessert if I fail the previous day, and I must engage in 30 - 45 minutes of exercise, such as vigorous walking.

Obstacles: These include: my love of fast food, a desire to get out of the home-office (buying lunch is a great excuse), my love of desserts, and a tendency to engage in serial eating when I'm bored.

<u>Strategies</u>: Take lunches in the nearby park and/or the beach; pursue new hobbies (indoors and outdoors) to avoid boredom.

Mental: Long-Term Goal: *Earn $10,000 in the next three months by acquiring new business.*

Medium-Term Goal: Earn $3,500 per month by devoting 20 hours per week to new client acquisition, and logging at least 20 billable hours per week.

<u>Short-Term Goal</u>: Devote four hours per day to new client acquisition, and log at least 4 billable hours per business day.

<u>Shorter-Term Reward</u>: Put $5 per day into a special vacation account.

<u>Long-Term Reward</u>: Take two, one-week vacations per year.

<u>Correction</u>: No time allowed in chat rooms the next day if I don't devote the appropriate time to marketing and writing.

<u>Obstacles</u>: I tend to look at the short-term, and forget the bigger picture, especially when money is coming in.

<u>Strategy</u>: Calculate current and projected revenues on a daily basis to avoid complacency.

Emotional: <u>Long-Term Goal</u>: *In three months, I will never again experience "dull moments," because I'll be pursuing one new indoor hobby and one new outdoor hobby.*

Medium-Term Goal: After repairing my bicycle, take a five-mile (minimum) bike ride at least twice a week; after upgrading to the latest version of *Civilization*, play the game whenever I'm trapped inside.

<u>Short-term Goal</u>: Engage in a new or existing hobby for at least 60 minutes a day, instead of watching television or eating.

Reward: The joy of pursuing the activity is its own reward.

Long-Term Reward: Buy new equipment for one or more hobbies – e.g., bicycle, golf clubs, gardening tools, software, etc.

Correction: If no hobby is pursued the previous day, I must perform a major chore the next day – something I'd normally do on the weekends.

Obstacles: Lifelong habit of getting stuck in routines, and then compensating for the boredom with food and booze.

Strategies: Attend AA meetings and remind myself to pursue my hobbies when I seem to be falling back into couch potato routines.

Spiritual: Long Term Goal: *Allow the Tao to guide my actions within three months.*

Medium-Term Goal: Read and reflect on seven verses of the Tao per week. (Note: I will have read the entire book twice by doing this.)

Short-Term Goal: Read and reflect on one verse of the Tao per day.

Reward: Ask the universe for a favor.

Long-term Reward: Attend a live lecture by Wayne Dyer or another "Master of the Tao."

Correction: Re-read one verse of the Tao if I fail.

Obstacles: See obstacles listed under "Emotional."

Strategy: Remind myself to read one verse each night.

Some of you might find it weird than I didn't list "abstaining from alcohol" among my long-term goals. This certainly was (and is) a long-term goal, it didn't make the list for several reasons. For one thing, even before meeting Dr. Lieber, I was enrolled in AA – a program that offers tools similar to those used in the perception modification program. I have a sponsor that I can turn to for advice and comfort, as well as group discussions that focus on life lessons and gifts acquired from past experiences. In addition, the 12 Steps offer a ready-made set of goals, along with methods for overcoming obstacles and challenges.

The fact of the matter was that drinking was no longer a problem – not at this point. And one of the main reasons it was *not* a problem was because I was using the perception modification program to uncover and resolve the issues that had fueled my drinking. More important, because the program was helping me to design a new Best Self, I was becoming a person who had no desire to drink.

Yes, my former self had goals, but they were vague and grandiose goals. I had few short- and medium-term goals (realistic ones). When I confronted obstacles and challenges, I rarely developed strategies for overcoming them. Instead, I compensated for any failures by anaesthetizing my feelings of anger, frustration and sadness with alcohol. I had been like a kayaker, struggling upstream against the rapids without a paddle. Not only did I not have the tools needed to achieve my grandest visions, I didn't even have the tools needed to achieve my everyday goals. I struggled to become an overnight success in one gigantic leap instead of following the methods taught by Dr. Lieber. These methods are premised on the wisdom found in these verses of the Tao:

> *Take on difficulties while they are still easy;*
> *Do great things while they are still small.*
> *The sage does not attempt anything very big,*
> *And thus achieves greatness.*

After reviewing my goals, Dr. Lieber and I agreed that it was time to move forward.

"Now that you have clear-cut goals, it's time to put your plan into action," said Dr. Lieber. "Be sure you actually implement your rewards and 'corrective actions.' (Previously, we were using the term 'restrictions,' but at this point, I think the terms 'correction' or 'corrective action' are more appropriate.) If you didn't achieve a daily goal yesterday, then you will take x corrective action today to compensate.

"If I ate too many calories the day before, I need to take corrective action to stay on track with my weight-loss plan. I might have consumed 500 extra calories yesterday, so today I need to exercise for 60 minutes as a corrective action, or exercise for however long it takes to burn off those extra calories. You could even break down your corrective action. For every 100 calories over your daily limit, you need to perform x minutes of exercise.

"We do *not* want loopholes, and here's why. People are very manipulative, and we're even more manipulative to ourselves than others. If we can figure out a way to talk ourselves into something or out of something, we will do it. So we need to take that potential for manipulation out of the process. We want our goals broken down so simplistically that we can't find loopholes any more. No excuses, no 'I was too busy yesterday.' Just do it.

"That's why it's so important for our goals to be realistic. We don't want to set ourselves up for failure. 'I can't do this. This is ridiculous.' Well, if it's ridiculous, set a goal that isn't ridiculous – up to a point. Don't set the bar so low that your only goals are breathing and sleeping.

"The only reason for not reaching your goals should be that you're not following your plan. The plan should be so clear cut that the only way to fail is to ignore it.

"I want you to be honest with yourself, and ask yourself. 'Can I do this? Is this realistic for me?' If the answer is no, then modify your plan. Make sure that your goals fit into what you want to accomplish, but are also doable. You don't want to go follow the plan for three weeks, and then give up.

"Once you can say, 'Yes, I can do everything here,' it's time to implement the plan. That is the commitment phase. Before we commit, we summarize. We revisit every exercise we've done to this point. Where are you today – physically, mentally, emotionally and spiritually? Review your vision statement, vision pictorial, goals, strengths and values, etc. Review all of that stuff again. Determine if there is still anything in your past that could complicate the move forward, or could be helpful in achieving the goals. Is there anything you've overlooked? Once you've done this, only one question remains: 'Am I ready to commit?' If so, you commit.

"We always set a commitment date. Very important. We've done all the work. We went through all the blood, sweat and tears. Now we're going to set the commitment date. I like to have clients set the commitment date about a week out. This gives you an opportunity to revisit your vision statement, vision pictorial, motivators, strengths and values, and all of your goals –fine-tuning things if necessary. Think about everything you've done. Go through it thoroughly. Make sure you've done the work and looked at everything you could possibly look at.

"When you wake up on the morning of your commitment date, that's when you incorporate your plan into your daily life."

PHASE 6: INITIATING YOUR PLAN

"A journey of a thousand miles begins with a single step."
—Lao-Tzu

Sessions #17 - 19:

In the weeks that followed, Dr. Lieber and I reviewed my vision statement, vision pictorial, vision board, goals, motivators, strengths and values. We also talked about the conversations I'd had with my support group, and (as usual) about the wonderful things that happened to me each week. However, since I didn't need to revise any of the exercises I'd done earlier, the sessions were fairly short.

One thing Dr. Lieber kept stressing was the importance of modifying the goals if I found myself struggling too hard. But I wasn't struggling. I'd just implemented my plans, and I was *very* motivated to see it through. On the other hand, I could see the need for flexibility. Otherwise, it would be easy to give up when the going got tough. After all, that's what most of us have always done.

"If you're struggling – really struggling to stick to your plan—it may be time to reevaluate," he said. "Instead of throwing in the towel, which we as a society tend to do, take a step back and determine where you're struggling. Where are you having a challenge? Maybe losing 1.5 pounds per week, or staying within 1,500 calories, is too difficult. Do we have any options that will allow us to accomplish the same long-term goals, but will let us tweak the mid- or short-term goals? Maybe adding 100 extra calories to our daily diet will help us meet our weight-loss goal – albeit more slowly. Maybe we should add more daily exercise.

"We can always make adjustments, if necessary. What we *don't* do is cop out. We don't make excuses. We find alternate ways to achieve the same goals.

"I also strongly recommend that you journal your progress. This allows you to keep track of what's happening. Should you step on the scale every day? Probably not. Once a week is fine, because it tells you where you are and how much progress you've made. Journaling helps you identify the challenges with which you're struggling, and identify ways to modify your plan.

"As you become more masterful, you'll start to see things differently. Over time, you'll awaken with more gratitude each morning, and a growing desire to serve others. You'll be more joyful, compassionate and empathetic. Instead of waiting for each day to end – to get it all over with – you'll wake up feeling excited, looking forward to each day's adventure.

"You are going to begin living your life to the fullest."

As it turned out, I *did* need to make minor adjustments to some of my goals in the weeks that followed. Trying to lose 20 pounds in three months proved too ambitious. By the end of the first week of dieting, I was hungry all the time. Then, when the first Saturday arrived, I pigged out, and didn't take corrective action the next day. Needless to say, this wasn't good. And rather than incur Dr. Lieber's wrath at our final session, I decided to adjust my long-term goal to losing 10 pounds in three months. *That* was much easier to accomplish, and I'm proud to say that I met this goal ahead of schedule.

The mental goal was trickier. By the time of my start date, it was late spring – usually a slow period for freelance work, and this year was no exception. Although I stuck to my short- and medium-term plans, I fell short of my 90-day revenue target. The work simply wasn't there. So, I analyzed my revenues for the previous two years, breaking everything down into quarterly segments. This led me to realize that my original goal was unrealistic. I was trying to increase monthly revenues by about 25%, and few companies experience that kind of growth without launching a big marketing push or a new product.

I decided to lower the bar to an average quarterly increase of 10%. This was still ambitious, but much more doable. Since then, I've twice met my new long-term goal of generating $3,000 per quarter, and Laura and I are planning a cruise to New England.

PHASE 7:
MAINTAINING OPTIMAL WELLNESS

"To the giver comes the fullness of life; to the taker, just an empty hand."—Lao-Tzu

Session #20:

In this session, Dr. Lieber reminded me (for the umpteenth time) to make adjustments in my plans, as needed, and to also remember that:

+ What we project outward is what we attract toward us.
+ We must empty the vessel, so we may receive.
+ Nothing stays static. Everything is always changing.
+ This is a continual process. It doesn't happen overnight.
+ This is your personal journey ... and yours alone.

Then he added, "Once you've initiated your plan, we have reached Phase 7 – maintaining optimal health. As you grow and mature, your goals are going to change, your direction may change, your Best Self and your visions may change. That is something we want to promote. I want you to continue growing and evaluating and reevaluating yourself.

"This is a continuous program. It's not a matter of reaching Phase 7 and saying, 'Okay, I'm done. Back to business as usual.' When you reach Phase 7, you may decide to return to Phase 1 and ask, 'So, where am I *now*?' Then you can move forward through all the phases again, because things have changed so drastically. Or you may end up going back to Step 5, saying 'My plans and goals have really changed. I *thought* that I wanted to be a veterinarian, but I realized that's not my passion. I want to join the Peace Corps.' Whatever the case may be.

"The process doesn't end until you're done with this life. But anyway, having been through the process for the last 20 weeks, what have you taken from it?"

I was speechless for what seemed like minutes, but it was probably just a few seconds. Then, without thinking, the words came tumbling from my mouth.

"I recently read about scientific study of the brain. It seems our brains send something like 10 times more information to our sensory organs than our sensory organs send back to the brain. The scientists concluded that our brains shape our reality more than *objective* reality shapes our perceptions. In other words, we *invent* our own reality, drawing any conclusions we want from our perceptions of life."

"That's what I've been telling you all these months," said Dr. Lieber.

"When that incident occurred with my neighbor, I could have viewed my arrest and incarceration as total disasters. After all, the whole episode cost me a ton of money and months of anxiety. But the moment I got out of jail on bond, I revisited the experience, and decided to draw a positive lesson instead of a negative one. It was a seemingly minor decision. But that little decision – to treat the incident as an opportunity to build the foundation of a new life – was the most important decision I've ever made. For the first time, I took control of my life. And I intend to keep that control.

"I've learned that life is ever changing and evolving, and so am I. In truth, my Best Self is who I am at this very moment. We are, and always have been, our Best Selves at every moment in time. It isn't who we can become that's important, but how we use what we've learned that matters in the end.

"We can plan and set goals and work toward those goals, but we must also embrace the knowledge that the goals we establish today may change tomorrow. Ultimately, we only have the moment in which to live. If we're lucky, we may find ourselves on a wondrous journey filled with obstacles, challenges and adversities. I'm not looking forward to more obstacles and challenges and adversities, but I'm not going to create a life that's designed to avoid adversity. Adversity teaches us great lessons. It's these experiences that give us life's treasures – if we choose to find them.

"The ultimate goal is to live life in the moment – to learn everything we possibly can and share our gifts. For me, that's the greatest gift of all."

So, you have now completed the program, what have you learned? The final lesson is the simplest of all. Do nothing. That's right, do absolutely nothing. Clear your mind and empty your vessel. To do so will allow you to receive life's greatest gifts.

Namaste.

ABOUT THE AUTHOR

DR. RICHARD POWELL is a noted naturopathic physician, doctor of clinical pastoral medicine, neuroscientist, health and wellness coach, educator and popular lecturer who has successfully treated hundreds of patients using his perception modification program. Dr. Powell holds degrees in Jungian Psychology, Nutrition, Naturopathy and Oriental Medicine, among others, and a former president of the Idaho Association of Naturopathic Physicians. Previously published books include the *Physicians Field Guide Toward Optimal Health, Supplement or No Supplement* and *One Body One Cell*. Dr. Powell lives and works in Twin Falls, Idaho, where he also enjoys golfing, flying and spending time with his wife Jennifer and his four boys.

APPENDIX

Phase One

Assignment One:

At the beginning of every assignment, list at least three positive things that have happened to you within the last week. For example: "I made it to work on time" or "I smoked less" or "I didn't yell as much." List whatever positive things have happened, and then re-read what you've written. This is an important step in early stages, because it helps you recognize that positive things *do* happen. Be grateful for all the positives in your life. Remember, a life without something good ends up being a life that is always ... not so good.

Seven Questions to Readiness.
(Please think carefully before you answer each question. And be honest!)

1.) Is life working for you?

2.) Are you happy right now?

3.) Are you being honest with yourself?

4.) If you were to continue in your current direction – if everything stayed the same – would you feel satisfied and complete a year from now, two years from now or five years from now?

5.) Do you constantly think that there is more to life than you currently have?

6.) If you have already tried other self-help programs, therapy, etc., are you willing to try a different approach to improving your life?

7.) If you are dissatisfied and ready to make a change, are you willing to surrender to life and let yourself receive?

Assignment Two:

Where are you right now in your life? Write a short story using fictional characters and your current life experiences. Who are you and where are you in life today?

Assignment Three:

Quality of Life Assessment

1. How would you rate your quality of life?

2. How satisfied are you with your health?

3. To what extent do you feel that physical pain prevents you from doing what you need to do?

4. Do you need any medical treatment to be fully functional in your daily life?

5. How much do you enjoy life?

6. To what extent do you feel your life is meaningful?

7. How well are you able to concentrate?

8. How safe do you feel in your daily life?

9. How healthy is your physical environment?

10. Do you have enough energy for everyday life?

11. Are you able to accept your body and your appearance?

12. Do you have enough money to meet your needs?

13. Do you have all the information you need in your daily life?

14. Do you have the opportunity to enjoy leisure activities?

15. How well are you able to get around?

16. How satisfied are you with your sleep?

17. How satisfied are you with your ability to perform your daily activities?

18. How satisfied are you with your capacity for work?

19. How satisfied are you with yourself?

20. How satisfied are you with your personal relationships?

21. How satisfied are you with your sex life?

22. How satisfied are you with the support you get from your friends?

23. How satisfied are you with the condition of your living space?

24. How satisfied are you with access to health services?

25. How satisfied are you with your transportation?

26. How often do you have negative feelings such as blue moods, despair, anxiety, and depression?

Assignment Four:

Take the Jungian Typology Test

Go to: http://www.humanmetrics.com/cgi-win/JTypes2.asp

Assignment Five:

Write one thing you would like to change in each area.

    a. Physical Health

    b. Mental Health

    c. Emotional Health

    d. Spiritual Health

Assignment Six:

What are your current challenges and what do you see as possible obstacles?

How are you currently working through these challenges and obstacles?

What are your motivators? Bottom line, why do you want to change?

If you had a magic wand and you could change anything about yourself, what would it be?

Empowerment, Confidence, Commitment, Change...

<u>*Phase Two*</u>

Assignment Seven:

Vision Statement:

Write a sentence or two to summarize what you see as your best self. Don't explain what your best self is. State what your best self is.

Assignment Eight:

Vision Pictorial:

Write in detail about your personal dream home and your best *You*, as if you were explaining your vision to your personal architect. As an example, I see myself at 135 lbs.

Be specific and descriptive. When finished, the vision pictorial should be a short story of who you want to become – told in the present tense.

Assignment Nine:

Vision Board:

A vision board is a collection of items placed on a white poster board. Each item is something that you want in your future. The vision board doesn't have to be finished in one day, and it might take years to finish (if ever). As an example, I see myself living in a brownish-tan house. It has three bedrooms and two bathrooms with a big backyard and a BMW in the garage. While flipping through a magazine, I saw the exact home that I wanted. I clipped the photo from the magazine and pasted it on the poster board. That's all there is to it.

Assignment Ten:

Which of your strengths, values and gifts can be utilized to achieve your best self?

Strengths:

Values:

Gifts:

Assignment Eleven:

Once again, what are your motivators? Why do you want to become this person?

Start a Dream Journal, a Daily Journal, a Daily Motivational and Affirmation Reading.

Phase Three

Assignment Twelve:

Write 3 to 5 experiences that have been extremely impactful on your life.

1).

2).

3).

4).

5).

One experience at a time, go through the 5-step process of objectively evaluating the experience. Continue working through each experience until you have exhausted all aspects of how it has influenced your life.

Assignment Thirteen:

Who are you now?

You've implemented some very powerful tools over the past few sessions that have impacted your life in some way. It's time to re-organize your thoughts to see where you are.

Re-write your vision statement and vision pictorial. Do you still see things the same as before? Is your best self vision the same? What has changed?

Assignment Fourteen:

List five individuals who are part of your support team. Identify the strengths and values of each person that will benefit you. Set up boundaries with each team member.

Phase Four

Assignment Fifteen:

Introduction to goals.

Write one short term goal for each area of your health. (Use the goal setting template below.) Short terms goals are typically daily goals. For instance, "I am going to work out for 15 minutes daily." My objective is to increase my heart rate to 130 BPM while exercising. My motivator is, my doctor informed me that I have a weak heart, and I have an increased risk of heart attack. My main challenge is, I hate to exercise. I am going to work through my challenge by setting aside the same time every day to exercise, and I'm going to begin by working out three times a week.

a)   State your goal.

b)   What are your objectives in accomplishing this goal?

c)   What are your motivators?

d)   What are your challenges?

e)   What strategy is needed to overcome obstacles?

Assignment Sixteen:

Write a mid-term goal. A mid-term goal is usually a weekly goal or a monthly goal.

a) When do you want to begin working toward this goal?

b) Set a timeline. When do you want to accomplish this goal by?

c) Work backward; establish smaller milestones toward the final achievement.

d) Reward yourself along the way. Reward yourself for a job well done.

Assignment Seventeen:

When reviewing your short-term goals, identify past experiences that may pose challenges to accomplishing your goals. List them, and explain how they could affect you.

Assignment Eighteen:

It's time to set some more goals.

Set long-term goals:

Set mid-term goals:

Set short-term goals.

<u>*Phase 5*</u>

Assignment Nineteen:

Back to motivators, strengths, values, etc. Put everything together into a comprehensive plan, and put that plan into action. Also, keep a daily journal of your progress.

<u>*Phase 6*</u>

Assignment Twenty:

Frequently review your plan until you have reached your goals. Periodically, take a personal inventory. Does anything need to be modified? Do you need to revisit any experiences (new or old) to see if your perceptions are accurate? Is there anything interfering with your progress?

Phase 7

Congratulations! You made it. You have remolded yourself into a new you.

One last homework assignment.

Assignment Twenty-one:

List all the wonderful things that you *are* and all the things you're grateful for. Put the list in an accessible place to remind yourself that when life seems overwhelming, you can accomplish anything. Review your current you. Re-evaluate your vision statement and pictorial.

Are you exactly where you want to be in your life?

How happy and fulfilled are you on a scale of 0-10?

How can you maintain your current quality of life?

Affirmations for Daily Living

+ I am at peace with the Universe.
+ I love and accept myself.
+ I am unique and loving, loved, and free.
+ I am safe and always feel protected.
+ I acknowledge all of my feelings because I am in touch with my feelings.
+ I am surrounded with loving, caring people in my life.
+ I am loving and accepting of others and this creates lasting frienships for me.
+ I trust my inner being to lead me in the right path.
+ I do all I can every day to make a loving environment for all those around me, including myself.
+ I am always connected with the Divine Love in the Universe.
+ My inner vision is always clear and focused.

Affirmations for Health

+ I have the power to control my health.
+ I am in control of my health and wellness.
+ I have abundant energy, vitality and well-being.
+ I am healthy in all aspects of my being.
+ I do not fear being unhealthy because I know that I control my own body.
+ I am always able to maintain my ideal weight.
+ I am filled with energy to do all the daily activities in my life.
+ My mind is at peace.
+ I love and care for my body and it cares for me.

Affirmations for Abundance

+ I am a success in all that I do.
+ Everything I touch returns riches to me.
+ I am always productive.
+ My work is always recognized positively.
+ I respect my abilities and always work to my full potential.
+ I am constantly adding to my income.
+ I always spend money wisely.
+ I always have enough money for all that I need.
+ I am rewarded for all the work I do.

Affirmations for Peace and Harmony in your Life
- I am at peace with myself.
- I am always in harmony with the Universe.
- I am filled with the Love of the Universal Divine Truth.
- I am at peace with all those around me.
- I have provided a harmonious place for myself and those I love.
- The more honest I am with those around me, the more love is returned to me.
- I express anger in appropriate ways so that peace and harmony are balanced at all times.
- I am at one with the inner child in me.

Affirmations for My Spirituality
- I am free to be myself.
- I am a forgiving and loving person.
- I am responsible for my own Spiritual Growth.
- I have given myself permission to be at one with the Universe.
- My strength comes from forgiveness of those who hurt me.
- I am worthy of love.
- The more I love, the more that love is returned to me.
- Love is eternal and ever-lasting.
- I nurture my inner child, love her and have allowed her to heal.
- I am responsible for my life and always maintain the power I need to be positive and have joy.

LaVergne, TN USA
18 March 2011
220615LV00001B/47/P